# Time Between

## The Hauntings of Cherry Valley New York

### By Susan Murray-Miller

"You cannot talk about ghosts and hauntings
without looking at the history
of a place and its people."

Susan Murray-Miller

Time Between

The Hauntings of Cherry Valley New York

By Susan Murray-Miller

Published by Plaide Palette Graphics

PO Box 464

Cherry Valley NY 13320

ISBN 978-0-9746558-2-6

Produced and printed in the Unites States of America

"Where is Cherry Valley? If we thought our telling would bring the world to see, we would stop here and now.
For the charm of Cherry Valley is its greenness, its seclusion, its pastoral stillness and quietude, its Arcadian air of unworldly rest and peace."

Harriet Beecher Stowe   August 1872

# Contents

All photos and photo illustrations were done by the author with the
exception of the photos on pages 16 (bottom), 19, 27, 47, 74 (bottom) and 123.

# Authors Note

This is a book about people who have lived here,
passed on and choose not to "go home."

Please respect the people included
in this book and their property.
They have graciously related their experiences
and history about their homes, former homes,
businesses, family, friends and acquaintances.

At Cherry Valley  12  June 2012

"To fear life and its many mysteries
is to deny God and his universal creations."
Susan Murray-Miller

# ACKNOWLEDGEMENTS

I am so grateful to the people who shared their stories, their antidotes and their yarns. They are the true authors of this book. To the people who helped research, proofreading and guidance of which made this book what it is, my sincerest Thank You.

Everett Miller, Fern Whiteman, Jake Rury, Michelle Thompson, Bill Lane, Elaine Maier, Christine Walters, Spence Waldron, Ernie Ehlers, Judy and Andy Carson, Shari Ehlers-Rockwell, Don Judson, Barbara Duesler, Wolfgang and Loretta Welter, John McGovern, Ed Harvey, Rachel Osterhout, Jim Johnson, Lyman Johnson, Trista Haggerty, Linda Franzese, Ron Jamison, Barb Perry, Bob Whiteman, Wayne Wright, Frank Stock, Rob Earl, Pat Wingate, Zoe Smith, Shirley Guanu, Debbie Loucks-Moon, Jill Flint, Christian Henderson, David Cadwalder, Christine Erway, Dale Webster, Anna Spencer, Barbara hall, Tom and Bernadette Spencer, Stan Misiolek, Mary E. Miller, Tom Jolensky, Meredith Miller, Gary Lozier, Pam Livingston, Isabella VanDewerker, Bill Issacs, Joan VanDewerker, Jane Sapinsky, Jeremiah Newton, Lizzy Mott, Chris Peritan, DJ Cornelia, Barbara Barrett, Cindy and Jim Cotton, Mike Fox Sr., Sue Viscosi, Ginger Thayer, Steve Tines, Bud Perry, Mike Stiles, Larry Thompson, John Hart, Pattie Hughes-Yoerk, Cate LeBarre, Lisa Allen, Butch Yager, Leigh Harrington, Doris Sabler, Graham and Beth Hume, Pat LaFond, Dale Latella, Jonathan Graham, Sean Miller, Frank Sabler, Chris Graham, Brian Schermerhorn, Dianne Ciano, Elmer Baldwin, Charles Young, Evelyn Myers, Melinda Supp, Tom Garretson, Robin Healy-Bridger, David Melbourne, Patty Bartlett, Carol Goss-Bley, George Hade, Ely-Milliman, Marion Holmes and Bill Plymell.

"Many historical events, especially where there was trauma, remain as an energy force upon the land."

Susan Murray-Miller

# An Introduction

## To the World of Ghosts

The word ghost simply means the soul of a dead person; a disembodied spirit wandering among or haunting living persons. Ghosts have been around for eons of time and they remain a part of our culture, our belief systems, our heritage and our lives. Ghosts are forms of energy that remain attached to a place, an object or a person. These forms of energy get stuck between our physical world and the next world and can be sensed through sight, smell, touch, sound and by using our intuition. The more *tuned-in* we are to ourselves and the environment around us, the more sensitive we are to these forms of energy.

Some ghostly apparitions come to us in the form of recently passed loved ones, telling us that they are ok and they will see us soon. Others have been hanging around for years, even centuries, re-living their final moments, oblivious to those around them.

Ghosts stay in this place for many reasons so let's explore just a few of them:

- They might be severely attached to something or someone in this physical plane.
- They may be traumatized by their own death and don't realize they are dead. They stay stuck in the details of their death, such as in the case of murder victims, casualties of war, natural disasters or suicides. Just a small note on suicides, which are a form of killing and the universe does not look kindly on those who harm or kill another human being, including self. There is premeditated suicide where one chooses to die, plans for it and believes he or she will be in a better place (people who have terminal and /or debilitating illnesses). Then, there is the non-premeditated suicide, done rashly and with many regrets. These are the people that have the hardest time with being dead and remain here until their issue is resolved.
- Some are afraid to move on out of fear of judgement.
- Some have the fear that someone from their past will meet them on the *other side*. The person may have caused them great bodily or emotional harm while they were alive and they are avoiding an encounter with that person.
- Others possess great rage at a particular person or event and are unwilling to let go of the anger.
- And there are those who remain behind because they feel they have some important task to perform before they can truly go home to the other side.
- Whatever form or forms a ghost may take for whatever reasons, like people there are no two alike, for spirit is just an extension of who we truly are. We should realize that there is nothing strange or frightening about ghosts, for as Nobel Peace Prize recipient Marie Curie once stated, "Nothing in life is to be feared, it is only to be understood".

Now, there is one last and important matter to discuss and that is the fact that certain historical events, such as a battle will impart the energy of the souls participating in the event and the energy of the event itself onto the land. This is probably one of the most fascinating topics about hauntings and ghosts and the reason why so many battlefields are haunted many years, and in some cases centuries after the initial event. This is the type of situation that needs attention when releasing residual energy in order for the land to heal. This is especially true in Cherry Valley, where the energy from the massacre of 1778 still pervades many aspects of this area.

Although most people never become a ghost when they pass on, those who do never remain one forever. A spirit will eventually work out its ghostly existence and move on, either on its own, with help from spirits on the other side or from caring individuals in this physical plane. The spirit realm is our true home and a place we should anticipate returning to once our work here in the physical, earthly realm is complete.

And so, here are some tales of spirits, ghosts and specters of this area of New York State, an area of great beauty, timeless stories, enchanting mysteries and explosive history.

Main Street Cherry Valley can get busy at times, you just have to be aware of it.

# Echoes of a Haunted Past

## Phelon Mill      Redman's Mill      Rte. 166

All is silent on this starry night without a moon. The dew wet grass makes a swishing sound as we cross what was once an impoundment dike on the Harriett property. We are just south of the village of Cherry Valley and are visiting the site of the old Phelon Mill, abandoned now for at least one-hundred years. We pass two foundations that were once the houses of the workers who helped with the mill. Their foundations are filled with weeds. You have to know where to find them in the tall grass at the top of the mill run.

Then you hear it, the groan of heavy wooden gears, that bumping sound as gear teeth intermesh with each other. You strain your ears to hear the sounds that are unmistakable; the sound of an old mill wheel as it grinds wheat to flour.

This was a busy place, where horses hitched to wagons waited patiently for their cargo and the smell of grain, horse sweat and burlap once filled the air.

As one gets closer, the sounds of a working mill cease, replaced by the soft moan of the wind and the swishing sound of your feet moving through the grass. The mill building is now a dark lump in the field, a lonely and forlorn image of its former self. Built around 1830, this mill made a decent living for the Phelon dynasty who ran it from their home, Willow Hill.

The roof sags, siding is missing, tattered rope hangs limply from pulleys suspended from the ceiling and the huge millwheel is half-way buried in the mud. As you glance up, stars appear through gaping holes in the roof. This is a sad place, but sometimes you catch a glimpse of what was once here.

The mill is gone now, torn down in 2009 and relocated to a farm on East Hill.

# The Indian
# on the Old Town Road

The old Town Road used to stretch from Fort Plain to Cherry Valley. The road crossed several ridges and was a fast way to come into town from the northeast. There is one section that few people know about and this part is still as it was before the Revolutionary War when Indians used this trail to get from the Mohawk Valley to the western part of New York State. This small section is now no more than a walking trail used by snowmobilers and four wheelers. It skirts a narrow ridge and then crosses over a natural dam and bridge that holds in, what locals call *Sunken Lake*.

At the face of this natural dam is a large waterfall that tumbles down a ravine and into a gorge. It is on quiet summer evenings just before sunset as you walk quietly up the trail toward the sound of tumbling water that you will encounter *him*.

At first you hear a panting sound, faintly, like someone out of breath. You glance back; nothing. You turn to continue and the sound of heavy breathing is louder now, just behind you. The hair on the back of your neck stands up and a cold sweat breaks out on your forehead. You stop, turn quickly to confront the oncoming person; nothing. Then, as you stand there looking back a slight breeze hits your damp skin as if someone or something has just run past you, never stopping or slowing down to acknowledge you. You turn and glance back up the trail, but you see nothing. You keep staring and then a few hundred feet up the trail, almost to the natural stone bridge and the cliff face, you glimpse but only for a second the shape of a tall, dark man running. His head is held erect, body bent forward. He has brown leggings and his moccasin feet are silent on the rocky path. The feathers in is hair wave quietly in the soft twilight air and he clutches a long, slender rifle.

# The Carey House   Main Street

The Carey family built this house sometime in the 1840's. The Brien's purchased it in the late 1850's and the Dingman family, local green grocers acquired it in the 1880's. In the 1930's it was converted to the American Legion Hall and then, once again became a one-family home when the American Legion moved to the former Judd Iron Foundry known as the Village Hall.

---

"Well, I can tell you about the many things that have happened in this house and some of them were very disturbing, especially at the time they happened.
We bought the house in the 1970's. My mom and dad, my sister, me and sometimes my little niece would all stay here. Cherry Valley was a refreshing place to live compared to our old neighborhood in Queens.
My little niece used to play in the large, unfinished room that overlooked Main Street. In this room was a staircase to the attic. Now, the bedrooms on the second floor, of which the unfinished room is one of them, were all interconnected. You got from one room to another

by going into one room and through that room to the next room.

Things went well for a few months and then one day my niece refused to play in the unfinished room any more. She said that a lady dressed all in white would come down the attic stairs and just stand there watching her. It made her feel funny.

That proclamation did not disturb us too much until one evening when my sister and my niece were sleeping in the bed in the back room. They both woke up at the same time and there stood the *White Lady*. Both girls saw her at the same time and both girls screamed bloody murder. That incident seemed to start unusual events accelerating.

Items started falling off shelves, including books and sewing notions. Scissors and tools would be missing from their accustomed places one minute and be there the next minute. Shadows would flit across your peripheral vision, just enough to make you want to turn your head to see who was there.

One day my mom was playing the piano, which was in the living room. The bowl and stand that sat on top of the piano started moving across the piano to the edge. I stood there and told my mom to keep playing and that I would catch the bowl. To my surprise the bowl and stand floated off the edge of the piano and staying in mid-air proceeded to the center of the room where they descended very slowly and carefully to the floor. It was as if they were being placed there by unseen hands. My poor mom was beside herself with shock at the time.

It was then and there I resolved to stop this nonsense. I consulted my parish priest who supplied me with holy water and a house blessing. I blessed and re-blessed each and every room. Things quieted down, but just for a little while.

The next incident was when a friend of mine came to visit and not being of the ghost believing type, continued to scoff at all the trials and tribulations that were happening at our home. He was sitting in one of the chairs in our living room and was making derogatory remarks about spirits when the large tray, a special family heirloom from my Norwegian ancestors, decided to do something creative. The tray and its hanger silently detached themselves from the wall and floated to the center of the room. Then, they very nicely descended to the floor right in front of him. Needless to say, my friend was more than impressed.

The events at the house became so unsettling, I was afraid to leave my mother alone there during the day while I was working.

Out of desperation I contacted a Shamanic friend who came to the house and informed me that one room in particular was filled with ghosts, some of them my deceased relations. He proceeded to bless and smudge the entire house inside and out.

That quieted things down for a while, but to this day I am not pleased about the way those ghosts, for lack of a better word, made my mom feel."

F.S. Cherry Valley NY

# Barnum Hop Farm    Doc Ahler's House    Doc Ahlers Road

The house, hay barn and the hop barn were supposedly built by a Campbell sometime before 1850. The Barnum's, Cherry Valley attorneys bought the property on speculation and rented it out as a hop farm with much of the proceeds going to them. The farm originally covered several hundred acres and was a productive enterprise. With the decimation of the hops industry in the 1890's, the farm became a dairy and then in 1920, Doctor Ahlers, a local country doctor purchased the farm.

---

"My grandfather bought the house in the 1920's. He was a doctor. My aunt inherited the house and my family lived next door. Anyway, it was my aunt's house and there was always a creepy feeling in it. When I was a teenager (2001/2002), my father and I lived there for a time and I refused to sleep upstairs. I had a bedroom downstairs. After a few months I was encouraged to sleep upstairs and so one evening I made up my mind to do just that. Mistake! Things went along well for a few weeks and then, one night I woke up to the sensation of someone strangling me. There was this black figure on top of me choking the life out of me. All of a sudden five white figures appeared in my room (I still to this day attribute those figures to my aunt and grandmother and other family members who had passed on). Well, these figures managed to chase the dark figure out of the room. Whoever says that they don't believe in guardian angels and guardian spirits better talk to me, I'll set them straight. I had bruises that looked like finger marks on my neck for many, many weeks after that."
S.A.R. Roseboom NY

"I remember when my uncle passed and we were all assembled in the kitchen having a cup of tea after the funeral. The tea kettle was boiling away and the steam had accumulated as little water droplets on and around the microwave which was on the counter. We noticed these tiny human footprints in the steam droplets that had accumulated on the counter. These footprints led all the way up to and through the microwave door. We always asked Uncle John to give us a sign when he got to where he was going, and I guess he did."
S.A.R. Roseboom NY

I remember a particular neighbor of ours who literally was scared of the house. One day he needed to go to the bathroom. He must have wanted to go really bad because you would never catch him in the house alone; no way. There he was in the bathroom, doing what one would do in a bathroom and suddenly something shouted, "Get out". He did just that.

He rocketed out of the front door with his pants down around his ankles and we all had a good laugh."
E.A. Cherry Valley NY

"I remember when one of my sisters' little friends saw the ghost of a lady on the stairs in the house. That little girl took a bad tumble down the stairs after seeing that ghostly lady."
E.H. Cherry Valley NY

The Doc Ahler's home

"When we were kids, we were oftentimes sent down to the basement to get one thing or another. The basement had a pair of steps leading to the outside and these steps were basically dirt. No one used those steps as they were rather dangerous and one could slip and fall. Almost every time, while we were in the basement, this little boy about eight or ten years old would appear and he would sit on those dirt steps and watch us. He had slicked-back dark hair and he was wearing what looked like a school uniform. Most of us kids were afraid of him and it became a real chore to go down in that basement."
L.M. Schenectady NY

*"An idea, like a ghost, must be spoken to a little before it will explain itself."*

Charles Dickens

# The Bodies in the Road    Main Street

One comes across many stories and articles from the past and whether they are true or not seems up to one's conviction or the truthfulness of the storyteller; sometimes a little of both. Here is a tale that I thought was very interesting and the fact that I heard it from more than one person over the twenty-five years I've been here may give it some credence. Maybe!

It seems that in the mid 1800's when Douglas Campbell was still alive and in residence at his family home of Achinbrech, the village of Cherry Valley decided to improve the road in front of what is now the row of commercial buildings housing the café and the flower shop on Main Street.

Road crews were pulled in and the digging commenced to clear away many years of loose rock and dirt to get down to firm bedrock for the new roadbed.

Several days into the project a shout was heard over the digging and hauling noises. A pit was discovered and inside the pit were two bodies. The corpses were dressed in what one could conceive as white gowns, some with blue pin-striping and tall conical hats and much of the remains were mummified. There was a regular *people jam* at the side of the pit all wanting to get a glimpse of this unusual site. Who were these people and why the costumes? It was decided that they should be given a proper burial but who wanted to inter them? One of the local undertakers stepped forward and took charge and Douglas Campbell (1839 – 1893), great grandson of Col. Samuel Campbell of Revolutionary War fame came forward and offered a place in the Campbell family plot or just outside of it (no one remembered which it was) for interment.

Now, they were not sure of what happened next but it seems that as soon as the two bodies were hoisted from their "eternal resting place" they just disintegrated. All that was left were a few teeth and dust and of course the clothing, which surprisingly stayed intact. No rot could be found on it and as hard as they tried no one could rip the clothing and when singed with a flame the cloth would not burn. Hastily the clothing was made to serve as a shroud for the two bodies which were rolled up into small bundles and buried in the Campbell plot. Where in the Campbell plot is lost in the annals of time.

Main Street 1890's

# The Scott Homestead    Hawk Circle    Rte. 166

It was on this spot that in 1750 the Scott family made their home on a small farm consisting of one-hundred acres. On the morning of November 11th, 1778, Mrs. Scott and her seven children were in the home when the Indians and British soldiers came calling. Capt. Scott was on military duty that morning at the fort, two miles away. Five of the children were captured but Mrs. Scott, her infant and one other child were massacred and the home and barns burned.

Families returned to this land after the Revolution. They built a new home on this location in the 1790's which was replaced by another farmhouse in the 1930's.

---

"The original homestead is right behind the farmhouse that we use as a facility for our business and for student housing. The old barn fell down about six years ago but we had an historian in here who was familiar with barns and barn construction and he said it was built somewhere in the 1780's.

We used to joke about the vortex of trapped souls here on this land. There is almost a palatable energy doorway here where trapped souls live out their lives. It has a strong feeling of guilt and fear and I thought that this was associated with the Revolution but there's sometimes that I think this goes much deeper and is much older."
T.H. Cherry Valley NY

"We had a little girl ghost up at the old campsite, which was up in the woods. From the way she dressed I would venture a guess she was from the 1800's. The campers at our clinics were not afraid of her and she obviously liked them. A few years ago, we moved the campsite to a better location as there are a lot of old growth trees near the original campsite and we were afraid of wind storms and sensed a danger from falling trees. Well, I'll tell you that was one mad little girl ghost when we took her friends away. She seems to be rooted to that spot and will not move down out of the woods. She's still there feeling sorry for herself. I do take time to visit her occasionally. I just can't imagine why she will not go over."
T.H. Cherry Valley NY

British soldiers still come calling at the Scott homestead.

8

# The Old Flogging Elm     Alden Street

Our story would not be complete without at least some mention of the "Flogging Elm". The tree stood for over two centuries just a little south and east of the present-day Presbyterian Church. It stood within the confines of the fort on the property of what was once known as Woodbine House. It was finally taken down in the 1930's.

Why the *flogging elm*? Simple; this was where men and, in some cases, boys were given whippings for disobedience by their military superiors. One particular story is of a fifteen-year-old boy who, after going for a joy ride on Col. Alden's favorite chestnut horse was given twelve lashes for laming the poor animal. Up until the tree was cut down and for some time after you could catch glimpses of men being flogged out by the elm and on some occasions even hear the cries of the sentenced.

One of the last images of the "Flogging Elm" is shown in this photo taken in 1908.

"All a Skeptic is is someone who hasn't had an experience yet."

Jason Hawes

# Sutliff House    Main Street

Built by the Sutliff's in the 1820's and used as a residence by them before building their home across the street, the house became the home of David Nash sometime in the years 1858 – 1861. Mrs. N. Crune had the house in 1903 and William Waldron owned it in the 1970's. It is currently used as a rental for performers and administrators of the Glimmerglass Opera and is a pleasant home with a lot of character.

---

"Randomly I would smell this foul odor, something between sewage and a really intense, overpowering floral smell. When I smelled that smell the hair would stand up on the back of my neck. I was there for an entire summer with my kids. It didn't happen all the time, but when it did it was very uncomfortable. I checked and checked but nowhere could I find where that horrible odor came from. I even had the landlord over twice and a septic company in but no one found anything."

P.H.   Columbus OH

"This is our residence for the summer and I always felt a little uncomfortable there by myself. One day, just this past year I decided to confront whatever was making me feel this way. I stood in the middle of the room downstairs and just said "who are you and leave me alone. I don't like the way you make me feel." After that I wasn't bothered anymore and it became quite pleasant to live here."

E.F.M.   Colorado Springs CO

"I went to the house to check it out and make sure everything was in order as I was very perplexed after getting housing reviews about the place being haunted. I took my friend, Rose with me. Now, Rose does not like to come to Cherry Valley as she is very sensitive in a psychic sort of way and she is constantly saying to me "Cherry Valley scares me." We went into the house and the first thing that happens is the kitchen door keeps opening and closing on its own. The door knob would turn, the door would open right while we stood there but no one was on the other side of the door. Rose quietly hurried out and sat in my car while I finished the rest of my house inspection. We left about half hour later and she didn't speak to me the entire way home."

D.C. Cooperstown NY

"My car keys were constantly in a state of *missing*, so I had to learn to stand in the middle of the kitchen and demand, at no one in particular, my keys back. I would leave the room for five minutes and when I came back the keys would be on the counter where I left them in the first place. I know this sounds silly, but what is even funnier is that one of my roommates slept with her keys under her pillow."

E.R-R. Chicago IL

"I have never been in a haunted house before let alone lived in one, so it was a new experience for me and I must admit an intriguing and pleasant one. They warned me but until you actually live in a haunted house you just can't imagine. I feel I am a better person for the experience although it certainly wasn't something I expected."

A.L. San Diego CA

The Sutliff House on Main Street

"Why should I be out of mind because
I am out of sight? I am but waiting for you,
for an interval, somewhere very near,
just around the corner. All is well."

Rosamunde Pilcher

# Spencer Farm  East Hill

Settled in 1805 by Jabez Spencer, the original cabin was down by the creek that runs through the south edge of the property. Outgrowing that structure, the next building to be built was a home to the left of the driveway, near the main road. The permanent house, the first frame house in the area west of Albany was built in back of where the barns are standing now.

---

"I love to walk in the orchard up there, it is a peaceful place and, on several occasions, I have seen the figure of a man walking in the orchard near me. He carries a small pruners, one which you would carry while trimming dead wood from trees."
S.M-M.  Cherry Valley NY

"When I go up there to mow and bale hay I find it very peaceful to be there. My ancestors settled this land and I guess they are still watching over it."
T.S.  Cherry Valley NY

"My garden is where the old homestead used to sit. Countless times, while harvesting vegetables I have felt people working right along with me in that garden. There is no one there except me, but still that feeling of not being alone is intense."
B.S.  Cherry Valley NY

William C. Spencer still enjoys tending to his orchard at the old homestead.

# School Number 22     Kniskern Road

I walk along the old Kniskern Road, once a main thoroughfare for horse and buggy. The road borders the State Lands and becomes a rabbit-warren of old logging roads and abandoned roads that crisscross one another. A school stood in the clearing at the corner of this road where a short path to the swamp intersects it. That was over a hundred years ago. A close friends' mother-in-law taught here once, many years ago.

Sometimes on a late summer afternoon, as sunlight filters through the trees you can hear distant laughter. Maybe you could even catch a glimpse of a little girl with sunlight glinting from her bouncing hair as she runs in the meadow near to where the school used to be. This is a quiet place, a place of memories and dreams.

School 22 is occasionally still in session on Kniskern Road.

*"It's easier to dismiss ghosts in the daylight."*

*Patricia Briggs*

# Stay The Night...?

## The Susan Belcher House  Limestone Mansion
### Main Street

Susan was the oldest daughter of Abraham Roseboom, a noted land baron and rail road speculator in the area. The Roseboom family has had a presence here since before the American Revolution. Abraham owned over two-thousand acres of land in Cherry Valley and Roseboom in the early 1800's.

Susan married Moses Belcher in 1832. Moses was a local merchant and he and Susan ran a store on the corner of Alden and Main Streets in the Village of Cherry Valley right where the Community health Center stands now. Moses died in 1841 and left Susan to run their general store and take care of three small children.

Susan's father died in 1867, leaving Susan and her son, Abraham a substantial fortune in rail road stocks and land. One year later, Elizabeth McLean married Abraham Belcher and the plans were formulated to construct a home befitting their new social status in Cherry Valley society. Abraham Belcher, at the time was suffering from very poor health but even that did not deter him from continuing to build the house now known as *Limestone Mansion.* Construction started on the house between 1869 – 1872, on the site of the old Eagle Hotel, which was destroyed by fire in 1866.

Abraham Belcher's health took a drastic turn for the worse and he died of consumption (tuberculosis) in 1872, before the house was finished. His one and only child, a daughter, Mary Louise was not quite a year old at the time of his death. Mary grew up happily under the care and supervision of her mother, grandmother and her beloved *Aunt Lizzy*, Susan Belcher's unmarried daughter.

Mary Belcher became the first wife of Doctor Nathaniel Yates. Mary was twenty-five years old when she died of asthenia, a combination of typhoid fever and heart and liver failure in the upstairs room of the house. It was a gruesome death and Doctor Yates watched in helplessness as his wife passed away. Mary died three days before her first wedding anniversary and their daughter Florence was only one month old.

Florence was given to her grandmother Elizabeth to raise. Her step-sister Katherine, Doctor Yates's daughter by his second marriage also joined the family in the coming years.

Elizabeth Belcher died in 1917 and with her died the Belcher name in Cherry Valley. The house, over the years had been a rooming house, a recording studio and is currently the Limestone Mansion, a wonderful bed and breakfast. It has maintained all the character and charm of the original house including some of the ghosts who like to come back and relive those happier times and to check up on the occupants and guests in their house.

"There have been times when a guest has stopped at the door to the middle room and refused to stay there let alone enter the room, so we have to put them in another room. That has happened a few times but most of the time no one is bothered in that room and they get a good night's rest and a hearty breakfast. I think it's how sensitive you are to those things. As for me, I don't even notice and I'm here all the time."
L.W.  Cherry Valley NY

"When we first purchased the house, we took pictures in all the rooms. When the film was developed, what a surprise it was to see mist and orbs in those pictures."
W.W.  Cherry Valley NY

"I lived there for a few years and I just couldn't keep the radio from turning on all by itself."
R.J.  Cherry Valley NY

Katherine and Florence love to "check out" the guests.

Period furnishings and comfortable beds make for a good night's sleep at the Limestone.

"We had guests last year from Sweden who were here for the Opera. In the morning the gentleman came downstairs and asked us if we owned two little girl ghosts? I looked at him rather perplexed and asked him to explain. He told me that sometime during the night he woke up and there were two little girls at the foot of his bed. Beautiful little girls, he mused with long curls and white lace Victorian style clothing. They just stood there watching him. Before he could reach for the lamp on the nightstand, they disappeared. As he and his wife were having their breakfast I showed them our photo album which documents the history of the house. It took him no longer than one minute to pick out the photo of Florence and Katherine from the pages of that album."

L.W. Cherry Valley NY

Photos showing the mist indicative of ghost activity
were taken by the owners just after purchasing the mansion.

One Halloween, this is before it became the Limestone, we were having a party in the mansion. It was rather crowded and all of a sudden, I looked over and there was this man about to put the spindle down on an old-fashioned record player, like the kind that you have to place a needle onto the record. This guy was dressed in an old pin-striped suit and looked very formal and elegant and he had slicked back hair. The music started playing and someone made a comment on the music and who put it on? I said it was that guy and pointed to the corner where there was this cassette player set up, not the old-fashioned record player I had seen a few minutes before. The man was gone and so was the record player, but the cassette player was turned on and was playing music."
R.J.  Cherry Valley NY

"I was showing the place to some perspective buyers. This was before the current owners purchased the mansion. We were going up the stairs to the third floor and all of a sudden, I had this overwhelming feeling of dread and I couldn't go any further up those stairs. The feeling was so real it felt like I was listening to or feeling someone else's thoughts. They were of this man whose job was to keep the fires going in the mansion, put in fuel and do handywork around the place. He had just gotten notice that he was no longer needed. All this man could think about was where would he go? He had no place to go. He was devastated. It was as if these thoughts were stuck on this section of the stairs and I just walked through them. I also remember that his thoughts were also on the two women who owned the place and they were not kind thoughts."
P.W. Roseboom NY

"When I lived in Cherry Valley as a kid a friend of mine lived two houses away from the mansion. We would occasionally play hide-and-seek in his backyard in the evenings and sometimes we would hear a piano being played in the mansion. There was no one in there any of those times. It was really creepy."
P.H-Y.  Bogue NC

"When I'm asked "Are you afraid of the dark?", my answer is "No, I'm afraid of what is in the dark.""

Barry Fitzgerald

Elizabeth McLean Belcher still watches over her guests at the mansion.

"My husband Jim and I spent the night at the mansion with our baby daughter Sarah. She was only about two months old at the time. We had the room on the second floor at the top of the stairs, right hand side. Sarah was sleeping in a portable crib that night with "bumpers" that were to keep her on her back and prevent her from rolling over on her stomach. We put her into her bumpers as usual that night and went to sleep. During the night I woke up to the sensation of someone sitting on the end of the bed. When I looked, no one was there. Jim was asleep and I didn't hear anything out of Sarah, so I went back to sleep. In the morning Jim told me of a dream he had during the night. He said he woke up and saw a woman sitting on the end of the bed holding Sarah in her arms. She was dressed in Victorian clothing. He told her to put the baby down and go away. She did. When Jim told me about his dream, I told him that I felt someone sitting on the end of the bed too. We immediately got out of bed to check on Sarah and we were very surprised to see the way she was lying in the crib. She was totally out of her bumpers! She had never gotten out of them before and hadn't gotten out of them on her own again until several months later in her life! Sarah was perpendicular to her bumpers in the crib which was possibly the way the Victorian lady laid her down when Jim told her to go away. At that point we were convinced that Jim's "dream" was not a dream at all."
C. and J.C.  Conesus NY

# The Tryon Inn     Main Street

In the early 1800's the property was a trading post. It was owned by a family named Hall. Mrs. Hall was an enterprising woman and when her husband died, she and her two sons, John and Lucius kept the place going as best they could. When the sons left home, both at early ages Mrs. Hall began growing herbs, making tinctures and selling jams, jellies and remedies. Mrs. Hall was purported to cure warts and was affectionally known as "Aunty Hall." Many locals called her a witch.

Now, it was in the late 1850's that her son John began his association with the infamous Loomis Gang. John was a gambler by day and a horse trader by night and many times his mother provided necessary protection from the law-abiding elements of society.

The Civil War volunteers who were stationed at the barracks in town drilled on the property during the 1860's and when Mrs. Hall died the property was purchased by William Waldron with intentions of making it into a summer home. He demolished the Hall house that sat where the current dining room of the Tryon is now as well as two other buildings on the property. He planted extensive groves of fruit trees and called it "Waldron's Grove. Many picnics and circus performances were held on the grounds.

In the 1920's William's son, William C. and his partner Lewis Winnie built the Tryon as we know it today. The present-day dining room of the Tryon was the Gault horse barn and it was moved from the present day Schermerhorn property just up the road and placed on the foundation of the old Hall house. Another horse barn from another local property also was dragged over and placed next to it. Next, they partially dismantled and moved the old mill building on the Head property and that became the current *Guest House* on the property. The old mill was originally located next door to the Gault property which was a diner and gas station at the time.

Now, the 1920's was the height of prohibition and so the two partners set up a tea house. Not only could a wealthy family stay in the guest house in relative comfort but lunch and afternoon tea were also served. These folks came for one or two week stays in their big cars complete with chauffeurs. The chauffeurs stayed in what is now the present-day bar room.

A 1920'a picture of the Tryon Inn

19

"I never experienced anything and I would have known it but remember, the building sat empty for many years before the current owners bought it. You know how spirits love empty buildings!"

L.F. Cherry Valley NY

"I was at the bar when this lady came into the bar room. She nodded her head to apparently someone in the corner, pointed at the corner and said to me "do you serve special people?" I didn't quite know what to say to her but when I looked over in the corner no one was there."

T.T. Cherry Valley NY

"My sister was leaving for her trip back home. We were standing in the parking lot. I had my back to the guest house and she was facing it. We were hugging goodbye when suddenly her body went rigid. "Who is that person peeking out from behind the curtain on the second floor?" she asked. Then she shouted, "Oh my God, oh my God, I just saw the ghost!" She was elated. I am jealous!"

D.L. Cherry Valley NY

"I have a *ghostap* on my camera and one day I decided to use it. The kitchen area, the cellar and the bar all registered with activity."

"We have cameras throughout the restaurant and late one evening, while looking at the screens I noticed a green glow, like a green mist at the back door going out onto the loading dock."

S.L. Cherry Valley NY

"When I used to work there as a dishwasher the water faucet at the sink would turn on all by itself and then turn off."

D.S. Sharon Springs NY

"Several times I have heard voices in the parking lot but no one is there. It is like a group of people are having a conversation. You can identify it as a conversation but you can't quite catch the words. I wish I knew what they were saying."

T.J.D. Springfield Center NY

"We live near the Tryon and many nights I go for a walk with my dogs. Sometimes when I look over at the Tryon Guest House there are small illuminations coming from the windows; like candlelight. There was no electricity in that building at the time."

M.L.L. Cherry Valley NY

"I can look over from my back deck and quite a few times I will see a light on in the guest house. There was no electricity hooked up at the time. The light seems to go through the door and then I will see it again in one of the windows. It is not a reflection as reflections do not move like that. And besides, every time I see it I get a real creepy feeling."

G.J.T.  Cherry Valley NY

Bar room at the Tryon. In the corner is where the ghostly apparition of a man frequently appears.

"I remember when I first bought the place and I was here alone. One night the radio turns on all by itself and there was this song on it I've never heard before. It was something about angels."

D.L.  Cherry Valley NY

"My father worked there as a caretaker and he was always unsettled in the place, especially at night."

J.F.  Brooklyn NY

"I was a chef there and one evening I was passing through the kitchen and into the prep room. A very large, stainless steel bowl that was resting on the bottom shelf under the prep counter flew off the bottom shelf and across the room. It was like a *Frisbee*. No one was in the room but me."

J.G.  Cherry Valley NY

"I have been tapped on the shoulder, shouted at, talked to and felt various other sensations in the restaurant. I'm no longer afraid of it, I just try to take it in stride but I sure would like to know who these people are."

D.L. Cherry Valley NY

"At the last Cherry Valley reenactment, I was one of the British reenactors. My regiment was stationed on the Tryon Inn lawn. There were *suttlers*, selling their goods and the soldiers with their tents, guns and equipment. All that day we were drilling with our units and answering questions for the general public. The next day the battle was going to be reenacted so there were hundreds of people there. That night I was in my tent, sleeping away. About one a.m. I woke up to the sound of orders being given to a group of soldiers. I bounded out of bed and opened the tent flap and here is this regiment from the Civil War drilling right in front of my eyes. "Hey guys," I stated, "you're in the wrong period. This is Rev War not Civil War!" They all just disappeared right there in front of my eyes."

J.Y. Binghamton NY

"The first night we had the pool table in the back room we all played pool. After several games, someone scratched and so there were about seven balls on the table. We just decided that we would leave the balls there on the table for the night. The next morning all the balls were in the pockets and the pool cues were put away."

D.L. Cherry Valley NY

"Sometimes it gets really rowdy down here like a big party is going on and it's the middle of the night. We put the bar stools up on the tables every night. In the morning you will find at least two or three on the floor, sometimes more."

D.L. Cherry Valley NY

The Tryon Inn guest house. The Old Mill.

# Waldo Tavern  Sterns House  Main Street

The back part of this house was once the Waldo Tavern and it was originally built sometime in the very late 1790's to accommodate travelers on the Great Western Turnpike. The front part with the ornate porch is later and there is a tale about it being a bridal house (wedding present) as the ornate porch would not have been there when this house was a tavern. It was rumored that Mr. Waldo was a strict inn keeper and tavern master and a strict Presbyterian and had a penchant for hiring boys from the city to help him run the place. The problem was that many of the boys just disappeared.

Waldo died in 1807 when he was fifty-seven years old. His sons took over the business but both died in their twenties. The tavern became a private home after that.

David Sterns lived here for many years and even back then, his daughters told tales that were a little spooky to say the least. The tale about the man in the hallway is from those times in the early to mid-1850's.

In the 1960's the house belonged to *Miss Emma* and her sister Julia. They were two spinster school teachers and they lived there for many years with their cat *Stupid*. When they passed on it was sold to a faculty member of New York University.

The Waldo Tavern

23

"There is someone in that basement. It has been both recorded and filmed. I certainly don't know who but there is someone down there. They will move in front of you while you are walking down there; they just cut in front of you!"
J.R. NYC

"I remember when I moved in. Right about three a.m. there would be this knocking at the door. I would go down, open the door and no one was there. This happened several times and now I just ignore it.
Someone suggested that it just might have been a turnpike traveler from another era looking for a room for the night. Go figure!"
J.N. NYC

"The footsteps on the stairs were very loud and not so much that the person was stomping up the stairs but it was as if he had on a very heavy pair of boots."
P.S. Kentucky

"I have a wonderful picture taken by a friend of mine of a man standing at the upstairs bedroom window. No one was in the house at the time but the man at the window is definitely there."
J.N. NYC

"I remember my friend Ann saying that she saw a rather tall man looking at one of my photos on the wall. Within minutes he just vaporized into thin air, right in front of her."
J.N. NYC

"Once I was sitting in the back room reading and this orb came and just stayed there in front of me. This orb was the size of a basketball. An orb is a ball of light and it is considered the lowest form of ghostly energy, at least that is my understanding. Well anyway, I got up and followed it into the kitchen where it disappeared. I guess I am braver than I think I am."
J.N. NYC

"I got into the habit of locking my bedroom door at night after I realized that we had ghostly activity. I don't know what I was about to prove, I mean ghosts can go anywhere they want, right? This one time, just before dawn I woke up with a start. I was totally awake and alert and then this loud voice, right in the room with me spoke the Latin name of what I perceived to be the name of a plant. I was stunned to say the least. And so much for that blasted lock on the door."
J.N. NYC

# Story Tavern    Main Street

A Mr. Wilkins built the original structure, which is the back part of the house, in the late 1700's to early 1800's. The front part was built by John Story, a local miller and brewer for his son in 1812. The front was living quarters and the rear part of the house became William Story's Stage House with a separate entrance off the back.

This was one of the happening places on the Cherry Valley Turnpike. Court was held here and circuses and operas stopped and entertained the local population.

This was the time of the Great Western Turnpike and inn keepers and owners of stage lines were doing quite well, especially Cherry Valley.

About 1825, William decided to invest in the stage line of Thorpe and Sprague which ran their four horse stages from Albany NY to Cherry Valley. Story agreed to carry passengers on his stages from Esperance to Cherry Valley. Story sold his end of the stage line to John Wilkins in 1830 as the business proved to have more problems than William was willing to cope with. The tavern stayed in the family until the 1950's when it was purchased by the Fink family for an antique shop. Today the home is being lovingly restored and is a quilt shop.

---

"When one resides in this place it is a common occurrence to get up in the middle of the night to sounds of revelry, clinking of glasses and merry-making and the stomp of heavy boots on the floor in the downstairs pub area. We shout from the top of the stairs to "Quiet it down" and that usually is enough to get the noise level down and get us a good-night's sleep."

"There have been several incidents in the rear bedroom where two little girls are seen playing. Their presence is oftentimes felt in the afternoon. Many times, you can hear two women talking. It is very loud and it comes at all times of the day and night. It could be Mrs. Story and her daughter Anna."

B.H.L. Cherry Valley NY

"There was a little girl that died in the front bedroom. She if oftentimes heard crying. There is also a hidden staircase and an area where they hid slaves during the Civil War when this house was part of the Underground Railroad."

F.B. NYC

"Almost every night someone calls my name. My wife gets these cold breezes that go past her face. There is no excuse for the cold breeze and it happens in the summer as well as the winter. She has seen an apparition of this guy out where the old privy used to be. Me, I don't pay much attention to it."

G.L. Cherry Valley NY

Old Story Tavern, Main Street

"In June of 2012 my wife and I were guests of Gary and Barbara, who were the owners of what once was an eighteenth century pub located in Cherry Valley, New York. The pub's name was the Story Tavern and is now once again decorated in period fashion.

We arrived on a very hot day and the evening wasn't any different. After catching up on events, my wife and I received the grand tour of the house including the master bedroom where we would be staying that evening. A beautiful vase of freshly cut flowers adorned the dresser. Not too long after dinner we retired to our room for the evening. Being so hot, we had a fan running and the bed cover and sheet pulled down to the foot of the bed. Despite the heat we were tired from our trip from Vermont and expected to be asleep in no time. Around two am, I was sleeping on my right side on the left side of the fort-poster bed. I woke up when I heard what I thought to be someone quickly opening the door and saying "Hello" and then closing it just as fast. I thought I may have dreamed it and tried to go back to sleep. I was lying on my back and I felt the room turn very cold. Before I had a chance to reach down and pull up the covers, I not only experienced the drop in temperature but also felt an intense tingling feeling from the waist down. This seemed to last a couple of minutes then my whole body started to experience this cold, tingly sensation. Within a few minutes the room felt warm again and I fell back to sleep feeling more tired than when I first went to bed.

The next morning, I asked my wife if she experienced anything strange during the night. She told me she didn't. While I was telling her of my evening experience we both noticed that the flowers on the dresser were all wilted and dead."

M. and P.N.  Milton VT

Orbs are everywhere in the Story Tavern. Lots of activity here, and why not?
After all, it was were people gathered and it seems they still like to now and then.

"In every century, in every country,
they'll call us something different.
They'll say we're ghosts, angels, demons,
elemental spirits, and giving us a name
doesn't help anybody. When did a name
change what someone is?"

Brenna Yovanoff

# Prospect Hill House     Chestnut Street

The Whitbeck's owned and operated a hotel known as Prospect Point here. Built in the early 1800's, the hotel became famous on the Cherry Valley Turnpike for its hospitality and good meals and it had a reputation for supplying horses for every need. Until the early 1950's the building stood on the bluffs overlooking the Mohawk Valley, two miles east of the village. When the Cherry Valley *By-pass* came along it became part of our history. Today there is nothing left of the hotel or the farm and its many outbuildings except the beautiful view and hay fields.

---

"There used to be rumors about that place and how, if you were traveling the turnpike alone, just maybe you wouldn't get to your destination on time; if ever. There are stories of unmarked graves up there on that bluff. Horses were traded and merchandise was bought and sold, much of it stolen, or so the rumor goes. Anyway, a friend of mine used to mow that field where all those buildings were. Sometimes he would see things at night that he just couldn't explain."

S.M-M. Cherry Valley NY

"Our home was built on the back part of the old hotel property. My son was two years old at the time and he used to tell me about this little boy ghost in the garden, which was right outside his bedroom window. He sensed that the boy was very angry and very malicious and the boy carried a stick at all times. My son was very afraid of him."

D.L. Cherry Valley NY

# Bastian House   Lancaster Street

The Bastian family were local merchants and carpenters in Cherry Valley. William Bastian made his living as a painter and built his modest little home in the 1850's, right before he entered service during the Civil War.

---

"I remember when we lived across the street in the 1980's and I was friends with two children that lived there. The little girl always said she saw a lady dressed in a long dress at the top of the stairs. She was never afraid of her, she just appeared sometimes."
M.M.  Pepperell MA

"The present owner of the home, a great friend of mine had recently passed away. In the many times I have visited her in the house I remember she always said to me that you never could keep a light off in the living room. There always was one burning. No matter how many times you physically turned it off you would go into another part of the house and when you returned the light would be on. Soon after her passing I received a phone call from a neighbor and they stated that there was a light burning in the living room. I went up to investigate. The living room lamp was lit but there was no one in the house."
L.F.  Cherry Valley NY

"The house always gives the impression of being a busy place, comfortable but busy. No matter what you do to try to relax, there is always activity going on."
S.M-M.  Cherry Valley NY

The Bastian House on Lancaster Street is a busy, friendly, family home.

# Moments In Time

## White - Phelon - Sutliff House
## The Cherry Valley Museum Main Street

Built by Jonathan Kingsbury in 1812 - 1815, the house was acquired by George W. White, son of physician and surgeon Dr. Joseph White. George married Mary J. Phelon, daughter of eminent miller and farmer Joseph Phelon in 1833 and moved to the home. George ran a lodging and stage coach service on the Great Western Turnpike from this house in the 1840's through the early 1860's.

In 1867, George's father-in-law, Joseph Phelon re-acquired the house and it has been passed down through subsequent generations of Phelons ever since. In 1959, Grace Sutliff, descendent of the Phelon dynasty bequeathed the house to the Cherry Valley Historical Association.

The building is filled with some of the most interesting, historical items that one can come across in a lifetime. A walk through the rooms gives one a true sense of history and timelessness.

The interesting feelings come from one upstairs bedroom and the hallway into that bedroom. There is also rumored to be a young woman who sits in a chair in the parlor and reads and sews.

The place is always cool. The sadness that pervades the home is overpowering for some, disturbing for others and for the rest of the visitors and some of the staff and volunteers at the museum, just not noticeable at all.

---

"I always had an infinity for the old rocker in the parlor. The one that is late nineteenth century and the museum personnel don't encourage you to sit in it so they rope it off so you don't sit in it. Well, one day the temptation was just too much. Now mind you, I don't let into temptation a lot but just this one time in all the times I have been a volunteer at the museum I was going to do this one thing; sit in that chair. And being that it was a slow day and no one was around, or at least I thought so, I sat in that blasted chair. Now mind you it was not the most comfortable chair but in lieu of other nineteenth century chairs I have sat in, it was ok.

I was just sitting there enjoying the feel of the chair and looking at the paintings on the wall and envisioning what it was like to be back in that period of time when all of a sudden, I felt this weight on my lap. It was like someone was sitting in my lap. Now all I needed was for someone to come in at that moment and here I was being held hostage by an unseen derrière. Well, needless to say I lost it! All my brain was saying was "Get out of here" and my body followed. It took me hours to compose myself and so I sat on the bench; outside. I was so unnerved that I even had Barb, the curator go in and get my sweater and book I had left inside. I vowed then and there that it would be my last year of volunteering and I am saddened to say that it was."

F.J.W. Cherry Valley

"Oh yeah, I see her all the time. I see her sitting in the living room. She is a young person about early twenties. Sometimes she is reading and sometimes she is sewing. I've seen her on several occasions. You know, you look into the parlor as you go past the doorway and you see her. She is just sitting there in the rocker. You retrace your steps and make an effort to acknowledge her but she is gone."

S.M. Cherry Valley NY

"My son and I were visiting the museum last month and when we came out and got to the curb and started to get into the car, my son came over to me and stated that the place was haunted. He said he saw a lady dressed in a dark grey dress, a long dress. She had one of those white caps on her head, the kind you see women wearing in the late 1800's. My son said that he wasn't scared but he felt that she was very sad."

M.P. Roseboom NY

"It was the day before opening day; memorial Day weekend. I had just gotten home from the hospital and I needed to hang some pictures for the rest of an exhibit. After convincing my husband that I would be ok I sauntered over to the museum, turned off the alarms, unlocked the door and started to work.

When I came in I had yelled a greeting to Mary who is one of our resident ghosts. Mary never comes downstairs, she just hangs around on the second floor between the second bedroom and the small hall entrance into the *Weaving Room* exhibit. She never bothers anyone she is just there if you can sense those things.

I began collecting all the pictures that would be put on the wall for the exhibit we were composing. There was a tall stepladder for me and the heavy case that I would be working behind was pulled out and away from the work space.

I started putting the hangers up into the molding and placing the photos in their proper place on the wall. I would go up the ladder, hang some pictures, go back down the ladder, scurry out from between the case and the wall and look at my handiwork, taking note as to which photos needed straightening.

I had just moved the ladder toward the door and was hanging the last of six pictures. Down I went to look at which ones needed straightening. I was muttering something to myself to the fact that "one on left one inch up, third one from left down a tad…" and I stopped in mid-sentence. The photos were moving all by themselves. I looked around, shook my head, took a deep breath and blurted out "the right end one needs to go up a tad." And yes, the right end photo moved up just a tad. For some unknown reason I started to laugh and then I blurted out "Thank you. Now stay there and we will do the next set."

So up the ladder I went, hung the last six pictures as straight as I could and came down. Standing in front of the glass case in the middle of the room I started to direct the final placement of the pictures with a little help from a very nice spirit. As I was finished with the exhibit I knew that I was going to have to get help in moving back the heavy case from the center of the room into its final resting place against the wall. I folded the ladder and brought it out from behind the case and looked at my watch. It was ten past midnight. So much for that; I would have to get help from some of our big, strong men in the morning. Just then I noticed a movement out of the corner of my eye. The case was moving toward the wall all by itself. Goose bumps now appeared on my arms and my hair began standing on end. I took another deep breath and said "Thank you, thank you so much. Now let's see if we can get the end back against the side wall." Yup, you guessed it, it moved into position nicely and in perfect alignment with the wall.

Just then there was a tap on the door and my husband walked in. He saw the exhibit and then he saw the case that was recently in the middle of the floor back in place against the wall. I held up my finger and proceeded to tell him that I didn't move that impossibly heavy case, I had help. I then proceeded to tell him the story. Maybe it was our young girl just wanting to pitch-in for opening day."

S.M-M. Cherry Valley NY

The Cherry Valley Museum building.

The museum is furnished with many pieces from the early period of the home.

# The Smith House    Church Street

The Smith house was built in 1840 by Henry Smith who was born in Connecticut in 1790 and died in Cherry Valley in 1857. He was one of the local clockmakers and jewelers. He employed twelve men in various endeavors in the town.

Henry married Jane Campbell, a daughter of Mathew Campbell. They had three daughters none of which ever married. The oldest, Lucy was an artist. She was educated in Boston and taught at the academy in Cherry Valley from 1850 until 1862, when the academy closed. After that Lucy taught art in her home at the *Annex,* which was the old Cherry Valley Firehouse. The firehouse was moved from across the street and attached to the Smith house in the 1850's when the fire department moved to Wall Street and the building was purchased by the Smith family.

Eliza Smith was the second daughter and Mary was the youngest. The mother and three daughters all lived and worked in the Smith house after Henry died. Lucy taught art and her sisters made artificial flowers for women's hats.

In the 1950's when our memorial library was constructed, the house and annex were again separated and moved next to each other to become individual homes.

---

"My daughter would sit quietly on her bed drawing in her sketch pad. As she drew, she had this dawning awareness that there was someone else in the room with her. She would glance around but no one was there, yet my daughter could feel a presence and it was female. At first the feeling was a little unnerving but still comforting. It was like this person had taken a personal interest in her and her artwork. This would happen often as she drew in her room encouraged by an unseen mentor."

S.V.  Cherry Valley NY

"It was so distinct, "Hi Hun." Now I wasn't dreaming and it was loud. I couldn't help but notice. It woke me from a sound sleep. Sometimes I go back to bed for a short nap after seeing my husband off to work in the wee hours of the morning and that morning was no exception. I remember I glanced at my alarm clock when I heard it. It was 9:05 am. I usually met my cousin who lives next door for afternoon tea and I recounted the experience I had had. She quizzed me by asking what time the event happened. I told her and she got really quiet. She told me that she was washing the breakfast dishes and she distinctly heard the same greeting at the same time."

S.V.  Cherry Valley NY

"The former owner of the house, Eileen always said she felt comfortable in a house with all women. I never asked her what she meant by that but now I know she realized, more than most people about the house. She lived there for many years with her dog, *Puff* and her cat and she was most happy."

S.M-M. Cherry Valley NY

The Smith house on the left and the fire hall on the right
once were joined together as a home and studio.

The rear upstairs of the bank building.
The door at the far end of the hall is the door that leads into the original part of the bank.

# John Walton's General Store     Main Street

The Bank on the corner of Lancaster and Main Street was a bank from 1818 but before that it was the mercantile business of John Walton and Calvin May. John Walton originally built a wooden structure on the site in 1797 and it was replaced by the current stone structure a few years after.

The layers of time in that building are intriguing as well as unsettling to some. Either way, several people have had interesting experiences in the building especially upstairs. The back part of the bank was added on later but the stone part of the building is original. They used to store the prints and fabric and other dry goods on the second floor. The original floors were heavy wood planks. Cherry Valley Marble from the marble works on Railroad Avenue was laid over the floors when they converted the building to a bank.

---

"We used to have a teller go upstairs to read on her lunch hour. She used to say that there were spirits going by the door all the time as she read quietly in the corner."
R.E.Y.   Cohoes NY

"We were closing our house and my wife and I were signing the paperwork in the upstairs, back part of the building. I was following my wife up the wide steps to the second floor. I was taking my time going up the stairs and as I rounded the corner and proceeded up the last three steps I happened to glance down the hallway to where the door connects the old part of the building to the new part. Everything went crazy. The hallway elongated and the door changed from one that had no windows to one that had two window panes in the top. It was like I just went back in time; like viewing an old movie in black and white.
R.E.   Cherry Valley NY

"When I was young, in the 1940's I remember I would go to the bank with my father. I was rather a tall teenager and I could see through the teller cages into the back part of the bank. It always intrigued me that this tall man with a top hat would stand there in the corner by the stairs. I saw him on two occasions. He had chubby cheeks and wore an old fashion black coat with a white shirt and collar. He looked very formal. He was not that old, maybe late forties. I would glance at the teller and when I looked back at him he was gone."
M.J.M.  Esperance NY

The Bank building on Main Street

# The Old Sawmill    Starkville Road

Saw mills are pretty big contraptions. They have a large blade that sits in a wooden bed and then various belts are attached to a driveshaft and a feeder mechanism that feeds logs into the saw blade for cutting them into boards. Usually they are powered by a power-take-off shaft or PTO from a tractor. The really old mills were run by steam and water power. Here is a story from a friend of mine about a particular sawmill he had recently purchased from an estate sale. After he had it all set up in his barn he told me that he kept noticing the tall, shadowy figure of an old man standing beside the sawmill every morning as he entered the barn.

I told him to go out in the barn with his morning cup of coffee, sit on a bale of hay and get acquainted with him. He thought I was nuts.

---

"I finally got the mill trucked over here from VanHornesville. This particular sawmill is an Ireland made in Norwich, New York around 1920. It is very large and takes up a good half of my old dairy barn, but we finally got it set up and running.

We began sawing quite a bit of wood with it. It would run pretty well most of the time but sometimes it was so cranky that I would throw my hands in the air and go do something else for the day. Now, one particular day we had a run of oak logs. These logs were twenty feet and more in length and about three feet in diameter. I started up the saw and one particular log, bigger than most got loaded onto the feeder and started up the ramp where the blade would cut it into boards. I had the saw blade going at a rather slow speed as I didn't want to bind the blade. Well, before I could do anything, the lever that controlled the speed moved forward throwing the saw blade into a higher gear all by itself. I thought that it had slipped a gear and immediately put the lever back into the slot that afforded me a slower speed on the saw. Well, the lever jumped out again and went into the slot that sped up the saw. I looked around and shrugged my shoulders because now I was mad. I thought that a spring-loaded control on the lever would be impossible to move without human intervention. Boy was I wrong! That lever and I had what you would call a wrestling match. As soon as my hand went off of it, it would jump right back into the spot I didn't want it to be. After about the fifth time I just gave up fighting it. Well, the lever went into the faster position and when the log was just about cut through, the lever slipped back into the slower speed position like someone was guiding the saw.

One day, just after that experience I was sharpening the blade. Now you have to sharpen several teeth at a time and then rotate the shaft of the gear housing so the blade would turn and the next set of teeth would be on top in position to be sharpened.

I would have to get up and go to the control room and turn the gear each time I wanted to sharpen several of the teeth. I had finished sharpening the teeth at the top and was about to get up and turn the shaft for the sharpening procedure on the next set of teeth when the blade moved all by itself. I thought that a member of my family was in the room where the gear housing was and decided to play a trick on me. Nope. No one there, just me and the sawblade and whomever or whatever.

John's Ireland sawmill.

I must say that whenever I was alone in the barn where the mill was set up I would see something like a shadow or movement. I'd shake my head and glance back and nothing. But that unmistakable feeling of not being alone always put me on edge in the beginning. I got used to it as time went by and it didn't bother me as much.

I guess when I bought that saw mill and brought it home I just didn't imagine it came with an operator. I mean, I just don't believe in that stuff, or at least then I didn't. Now I don't know what to think. Anyway, I got a bargain; saw mill with operator. Can't complain about that and I don't have to pay him either. Double bargain."

J.M. Sprout Brook NY

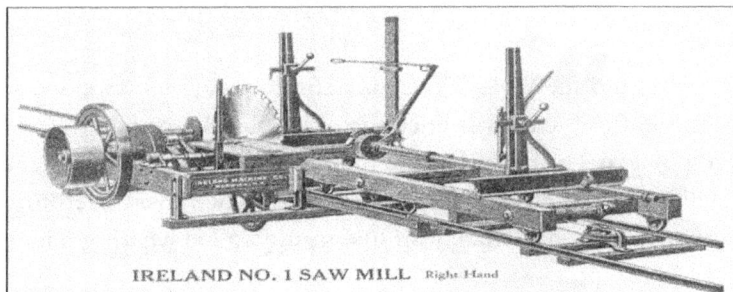

IRELAND NO. 1 SAW MILL   Right Hand

# Willow Hill    Fish and Game Road

The Well's House, as it is sometimes called was destroyed in the Revolutionary War and built upon its foundation was the sturdy home of Judge Ephram Hudson. After Hudson's death in the early 1800's, the home was purchased by Joseph Phelon and three generations of Phelons occupied the house until it was sold in the mid 1950's. An interesting story comes from this home that is worth noting. While cleaning out the attic for its new owners, the Judson and Phelon descendants came upon a framed, life size portrait of Oliver Judd in the attic. Oliver Judd was the father of Jane Judd-Phelon and a local iron smith in Cherry Valley. Carrying the picture to his home in Midland Texas, Mr. Judson decided to hang the portrait of his great, great grandfather in a prominent place in the library of his home.

---

"When my father brought the picture home my sister and I were just beginning our teenage years. It soon became apparent that there was something about that portrait that defied imagination. My sister and her friends loved to go into my father's library to read the old books he had, to study and do homework and occasionally they had *sleepovers* in there. Suddenly her activity in the library stopped and she would not go into the room by herself. She told me that the portrait was alive and that it had a strange glow about it at night and that the eyes would follow you about the room. Years went by, I got married and moved on. When my parents both passed and the division of the estate took place, not one of by brothers or sister wanted that portrait. I was very pleased to get it and I hung it in a prominent place in the living room of my home here in Texas.

One evening I had to go downstairs. It was about three a.m. and I noticed that the lamp next to Oliver's portrait was lit. I turned it off and went back to bed. A few nights later I came down stairs in the middle of the night again and I noticed that the lamp was lit. Once again, I turned it off and went to bed. The next time this happened I stood in front of the portrait and I told my great, great grandfather that if he wanted the light kept on he was going to have to give me a sign. Soon after that, Hurricane Ike devastated the Galveston/Houston area where I live. Power and services were disrupted for many weeks. Well, all but the lamp next to Oliver's portrait, that burned brightly all through the ordeal"

D.H.J. Midland TX

"The land around the Wells House is definitely haunted. Some evenings one can see strange lights coming from what was once the old orchard area where John Wells' sister was brutally murdered by two Tories during the massacre of Cherry Valley. A friend of mine has even seen a tall Indian standing near the driveway. The most unsettling sight is that of a very young woman. She is a small, waif like figure and is wearing a long dress and she seems to be looking for something. There is a sadness about her that you can feel. I wonder if it is the daughter of John Wells, the one that was killed and scalped in the front yard by a Seneca Indian on the morning of the massacre of November 11, 1778?"

S.M-M.  Cherry Valley NY

The Judge Hudson house also known as Willow Hill.

Oliver Judd's infamous portrait painted
posthumously by his grandson J. Story in 1878.

# Cole - Thompson House  Main Street

This house was initially built as a Judd House for the brother of Oliver who came with him from Connecticut in 1804. Oliver's mother-in-law lived here until she died and the Thompson's owned it in the mid 1850's.

William Waldron bought the house in the early 1900's and by 1930 Mrs. Cole, a school teacher had been living there for many years.

---

"My cat always knew there was something there. I did also but whoever it is has never bothered me. I would hear footsteps in the attic and of course the feeling of someone looking over my shoulder as I was doing laundry on the second floor, but nothing eerie, just comforting."

S.P.I. Atlanta GA

"I guess I better start acknowledging them or her because if I don't watch it I'll be going through boxes of light bulbs every week or two. They just love to play with the lights and burn them out. A friend came to visit and we were in the attic and he suddenly had to sit down. He said that he felt as if he had gone back in time. The attic, all of a sudden looked very different. He was disoriented and he looked ghostly pale. After we got down from the attic he felt better but he still would not stay overnight."

K.S. Cherry Valley NY

"This place is always busy, I mean you can feel the life and the hustle and bustle around you although you can't see it. I just wish for once I could just get a glimpse of them, just once."

K.S. Cherry Valley NY

Cole – Thompson house

# Sherman House    Main Street

Mrs. Sherman built her palatial home on the corner of Maiden Lane in the late 1860's. This house has a wonderful architectural style and has been added on over the years.

---

"I remember walking past one Halloween evening with the kids and there was a woman standing in the upstairs window. She had this kind of glow around her."
L.M.  South Valley NY

"While walking late at night I passed the house and there was a light in the upstairs window. The light had an orange glow and a woman wearing a dress with puffy sleeves and her hair in a bun was silhouetted in the glow of that light."
E.M.F.  Cooperstown NY

"We were having a picnic on the porch and my sister-in-law, who was in the house for a while came out and said she saw my lady ghost on the upstairs landing of the stairs. She told me she was wearing a long, turn of the century dress and her hair was up in a bun. I wish I could see her just once."
D.C.  Cherry Valley NY

Sherman house

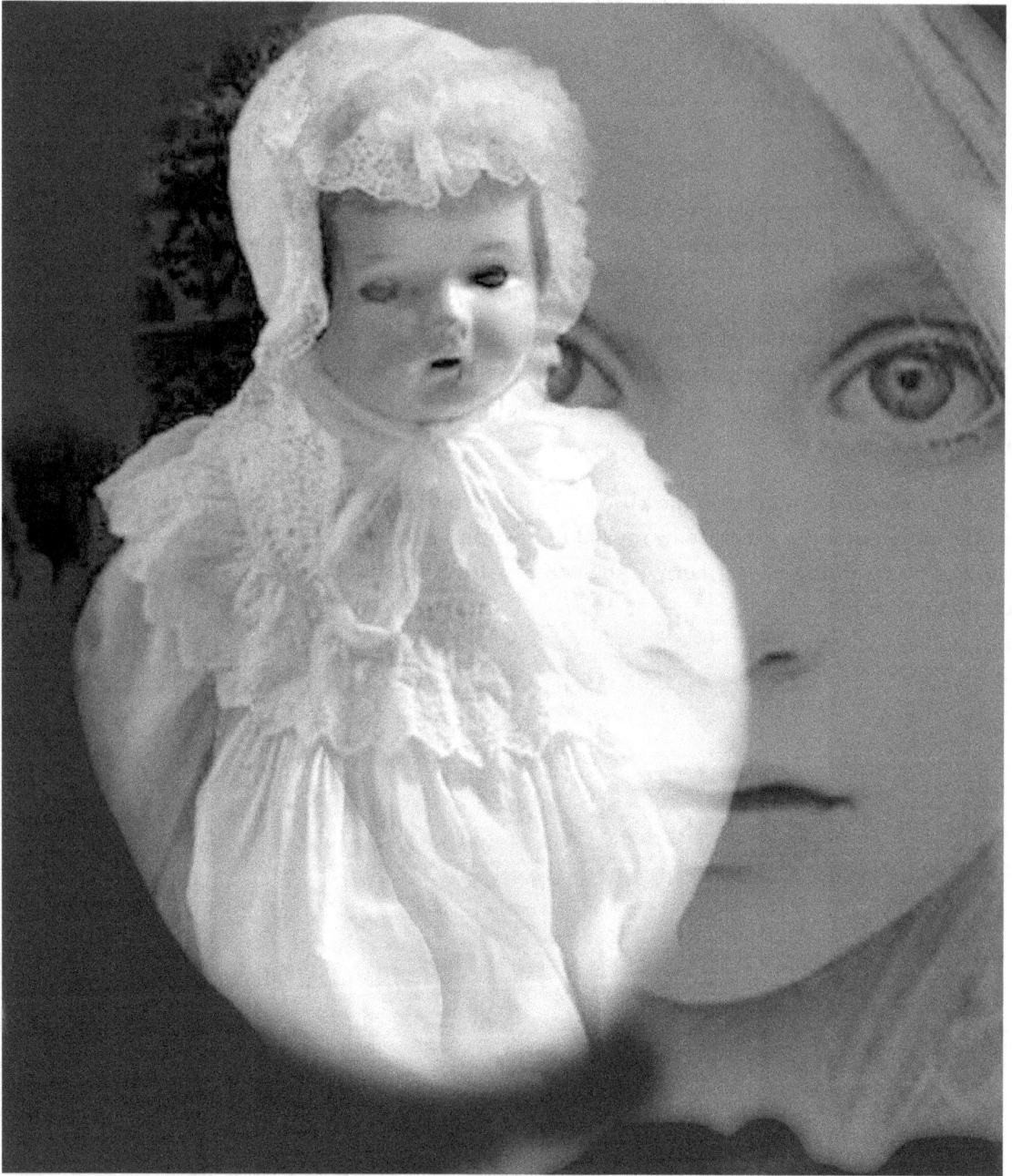

# Waldron – Chamberlain House   Lancaster Street

This house, one of many on the top of Lancaster Street was initially built in the traditional *Salt Box* architectural style and constructed entirely out of stolen lumber in 1858, or so the legend goes. Changed into its present architectural style in the 1940's the house had many associations with the Underground Railroad in New York during the Civil War era.

---

"My older brother was sleeping when he suddenly woke up and saw this little girl in his room. She was between his bed and the nightstand which is where his alarm clock was. She was just standing there looking at him. He saw the little girl's image plainly but he also could see his alarm clock right through her."

P.H-Y.  Bogue NC

"I had this little doll cradle when I was growing up. All my dolls would be put in there at night or when I went to school. My doll collection did have one antique doll that had a porcelain head, feet and hands and it was very old. Invariably that would be the one doll out of all of my dolls that would be moved elsewhere every time I went to play with them."

P.H-Y.  Bogue NC

We were members of the Presbyterian Church and one day, shortly after we joined the congregation this young man came up and asked my mom and I if we were the people who had just moved into the old Chamberlain place on Lancaster Street. We told him that we were and he asked if we had seen the little girl yet? He told us that he and his friend would be playing basketball in the driveway at our house and every time they looked up at the upstairs window there was this girl standing there watching them. His friend did not have a sister so who was the girl?"

P.H-Y.  Bogue NC

"The little girl always ran into the closet whenever we saw her. Now, what you have to realize is that the closet has a secret pair of stairs that goes down to the first floor. The legend is that a little girl of about six or seven fell down those stairs and died. She never goes to the first floor, she stays on the second floor and that is where you see her. You also hear her walking the hallway at night and she always wears a long, white nightdress."

P.H-Y.  Bogue NC

# The Cherry Valley Lithopedion    Dr. David Little

There is one story that I wish to tell within the confines of this book and I guess here is a good place to tell it. The tale is not particularly about ghosts but one we all should be aware of if we like Cherry Valley history and a little of the macabre.

Dr. David Little (died in 1832 at the age of 65) was a physician of notable repute in Cherry Valley and the surrounding towns. His daily rounds covered extensive territory and he made virtually all of them on horseback.

One day one of his wealthy patrons and a good friend, who happened to be a widower and raising an only child, a daughter called on him to take a look at her. His daughter was a beautiful and vivacious girl of about twenty years but she had been sulky and *under the weather* for several weeks and the father was concerned. The girl refused to see the doctor at first but after several attempts she gave in and saw him. Dr. Little delivered a diagnosis that greatly enraged his friend for he told him that his daughter was pregnant and that the baby would be born sometime in the spring. The father threw Dr. Little out of his house but not without one caveat; if she did have the child in the spring he would forgive the good doctor but if the diagnosis was incorrect he would make every attempt to ruin him.

Spring came and went and no baby appeared. The doctor was convinced that an illegal abortion had been performed but how could he prove it. Meanwhile his wealthy former good friend did everything in his power to ruin his reputation so much so that the good doctor's clients dwindled to a handful.

It was two years later, in the year 1816 that the epidemic of spotted fever in this area claimed the life of the daughter at age twenty-two.

On the night after her funeral, Dr. Little entered the graveyard and began the grim task of exhuming her body. This would settle the matter once and for all.

At midnight he started to dig and by dawn he had the answer to the mystery. The grave-site autopsy not only confirmed his diagnosis of pregnancy but resulted in a one-in-in-a-million find; a Lithopedion or more commonly known as a *Stone Baby*. This is a rare condition and occurs when a fetus dies during pregnancy but is too large to be reabsorbed by the body. The fetus calcifies on the outside, shielding the mother's body from the decomposing tissue of the baby and preventing infection. It is not unusual for this condition to remain undiagnosed for decades inside a woman's body.

Doctor Little wasted no time in visiting the home of his former friend, taking the grisly find with him. After many hours the two men emerged from the home, friends again to the last days of their lives. The secret of the stone baby was revealed only after the two men had passed into eternity.

The little stone baby was passed down to family members of the doctor and eventually donated to the archives of the Albany Medical College in Albany NY. In the 1950's the medical college donated the tiny package to the Farmers Museum and the New York State Historical Association in Cooperstown NY where it resides to this day.

The Cherry Valley Lithopedion
Note the tiny fingers and the little foot on the right.
Fenimore Art Museum, Cooperstown NY.
Photo by Arthur Telfer

The Cherry Valley First Presbyterian Church

# Sacred Ground

## The Presbyterian Church     Alden Street

The Presbyterian Church has had a presence here since 1740. In 1873, the present building was erected. It was designed by Rev. Swinnerton and funded by Miss Catherine Roseboom a local philanthropist. Through the years the church has had its share of ghost stories of which the *Grey Lady* is the most famous.

---

"I was cleaning in the back of the church. I had come to the church early, before I was scheduled to attend a meeting of the vestry committee in the meeting room next to where church services are held. Our organ sits in the back of the church in the balcony. I heard organ keys making a noise like someone was hitting them. I loudly asked who was there. No response. The same thing happened again and again, no response to my call.
I went over to the next room where the meeting was supposed to be and jokingly told them that they weren't being funny playing tricks on me like that. They all looked at me like I was from outer space. We all adjourned to the back of the church and our organist, who just happened to be at the meeting opened the door and went inside the area where the organ is housed. The organ stops were all pulled out and that is not the way our organist left them from the previous Sunday."

R.S. Cherry Valley NY

"I have always wanted to see the *Grey Lady*, but in all the years doing the work on the organ in the church I just haven't seen her. The church isn't a creepy place by any means, it's just very old. The lady is supposed to appear near the pulpit area in the front of the church and there are reports of someone playing the organ when no one is around. Someone else has seen her sitting in the front pews but that was a while ago. I just would like to see her just once."

S.C. Worchester NY

"The *Grey Lady* usually appears on rainy evenings. She is in a long dress and she silently glides across the street right in front of your car. You watch her walk to the church and then she goes right through the front door, I mean right through the closed front doors of the church!"

J.F. NYC

"I know there is a presence there. Over the years I have sensed it but never have I seen the *Grey Lady*. I can tell you several stories that I was involved in though. In the 1970's we had a preacher that insisted that we remove the railing from the front of the church where we receive communion. When the rail was removed things really started to happen; unexplained things. One Sunday just after we removed the railing, as our minister was preaching a vase of flowers on the altar just leaped off of its pedestal and crashed to the floor. Banging sounds and noises were plainly heard by a lot of people in the congregation at that time and it was soon after that the railing was put back in its original place. Things quieted down somewhat but she still makes her presence known.

Just a few months ago we hired a couple to clean the carpets in the church. The female member of the team was in the choir loft cleaning the carpets when she noticed a door off to the side of the area she was attending too. Thinking that it might be another room that had a carpet she opened the door and a voice, very sternly and loudly said "Get out of here." This poor and frightened lady screamed, ran down the stairs and out of the church and refused to go back into the building again.

I remember Gladys, an elderly member of the congregation always saying she believed that it was Miss Catherine Roseboom who is the *Grey Lady* because she always wore grey."

B.D. Cherry Valley NY

# The Mounds     East Hill

The mound sites are spread out in a rather wide area along a ridge line. Presently there are five mound sites and no one seems to know what they were used for, although there is lots of conjecture. Some scholars say they were places where ancient peoples placed goods for trade; maybe the traders on their way from the copper ore deposits in the Great Lakes. Others say they are burial mounds but that has not been proven. All that they do know is that associated burn pits and charcoal residue where giant fires were built point to a carbon date of 2500 BC. Four thousand years ago!

When you come up here there is a portal of energy that you pass through. You can feel the energy when you walk up the path. Your hair stands on end and you feel eyes watching you. After you pass through this energy field a sense of peacefulness totally envelopes you. You stand among these mounds of stones all neatly piled up and you wonder just why they were built. If you look for them they are just visible on the surface, but you know that at one time these stone mounds were at least four to five feet tall. All I know is that this spot among the pines and birch high on a mountaintop has a very sacred feel to it.

---

"I lived just south of the mounds and I used to walk the mile or so to the path and then into the site. It was always peaceful up there. I always had the feeling the site was very old. Anyway, there were times I used to look out my kitchen window and sometimes there would be this Indian staring at me through the glass. It was very frightening at first but I realized that he couldn't hurt me and I prayed for him."

V.R.A.  Cherry Valley NY

"Since I bought the property there have been numerous incidents, some very unsettling and others very calming. My son heard this ungodly scream from the direction of the mounds one night. The hair on the back of his neck stood up. It was a scream of such eeriness that he couldn't fall back asleep. It was not the scream of an animal he had ever heard before and he has heard most of them on the remote spot on our property where he lives."

B.H.P.  Cherry Valley

"I hunt up there and it is quite peaceful. Nothing has ever happened to me up there. I don't see anything out of the ordinary and I probably wouldn't see it if it hit me on the head. I don't see those things."

R.P.  Cherry Valley NY

"I remember the second time I visited. I was going up to celebrate the solstice with some friends and it was late afternoon. I saw these shadowy figures of people coming at me. They were walking toward me from out of the trees; through the trees. I stood my ground. They all looked at me and just disappeared. I think they were just checking us out."
D.P.B. Rensselaer NY

"One time a rather tall Indian walked right through our living room. He just walked through one wall and out the opposite wall. I looked at my daughter, she looked at me and we both laughed. We have to put some brevity on a situation like that or we would go mad."
B.H.P. Cherry Valley NY

"One day while I was walking up at the mound site I saw hundreds of orbs of light all just darting and floating around me. After a few minutes they all disappeared and that strange feeling of total peace was there. I find it a great place to meditate."
S.M-M. Cherry Valley NY

"When you step outside after dark there is an underlying feeling of someone watching you. It doesn't bother me anymore but it was very disquieting at first."
B.H.P. Cherry Valley NY

Orbs are everywhere up at the mound sites. Here they follow Peter and Sean up the path.

Sometimes a mound is hard to spot. They might look like a stone wall but upon closer examination they look like stone piles. There is usually more than one and they are in a formation or pattern. The largest site on East Hill has over forty-five individual mounds associated with it. The largest single mound was just discovered on the ridge opposite the East Hill mounds. That mound measures twenty-two feet wide and one-hundred feet long.

# Cherry Valley Cemetery    Alden Street

The Cherry Valley Cemetery is now within the confines of what was once Fort Alden. The fort was a large structure as most forts go and the actual cemetery grounds are now little more than half of what was once the fort. Contrary to popular belief, the fort was alive and well during the French and Indian War (1754 – 1763). The structure was smaller then but it did enclose the church and the meeting hall within its walls. When Col. Alden came here in 1778, he rebuilt the fort around the original stockade.

---

"Well I remember the tale of Alden's grave very well. My grandfather used to tell the story to my brother and I. Colonel Alden was massacred at the Cherry Valley Massacre in 1778 and given a very speedy, military burial just inside the gates of the fort on November 12. It was minutes before the second attack on the settlement. There was no time for a coffin, they just wrapped him in blankets and buried him. Colonel Samuel Clyde, a Revolutionary War hero from Cherry Valley died in 1790 at the age of fifty-eight and was buried in the plot next to where Colonel Alden was buried.

Our great, great grandfather was a part time grave digger and he worked in the cemetery when needed. Well, the year was 1824 and Mrs. Samuel Clyde had just passed and they were to bury her next to her husband. This would place her between her husband, Colonel Samuel and Colonel Alden.

They started digging and things were well underway when a shout was heard from the bottom of the grave. The two men in the grave were almost down to six feet deep at the time. Suddenly, the wall of Colonel Alden's grave collapsed. The two men in the pit were showered with dirt and debris and the skeleton of Colonel Alden.

After extracting the men and making sure they were all right, they turned their attention to Alden's body. They all viewed the tomahawk mark in the skull where he was scalped and after much debate about giving him a coffin for a proper burial, it was decided to put him back the way he was originally interred. The body was carefully and reverently wrapped up, a minister was dispatched and Colonel Alden was placed back in his eternal resting place. Boards were fetched and a wall was placed between the two graves. Mrs. Clyde could rest in peace and so could Colonel Alden.

Oh, my grandfather just happened to mention that one of Alden's teeth fell out and great grandfather retrieved it. He kept it in a special jar. I know my father had it at one time, darned if I know there it is now."

G.T.  Cherry Valley NY

"I go into the cemetery to place flowers on the graves of my mom and dad, my husband and my son and then I go. I don't roam around like I used to do when I was younger. Too many times I have gone through cold spots, have had my cheek lightly caressed or my hair pulled. Nope, no more. Do my duty and then I'm out of there."

L.C.F. Cherry Valley NY

"My daughter was walking through the cemetery, as she often did in the afternoon. She was pushing her eighteen-month old daughter in her stroller. When she approached the old part of the cemetery my granddaughter started to giggle and wave at something or someone that was obviously there but my daughter couldn't see anyone. Then my granddaughter started throwing kisses. There was absolutely no one there. As my daughter stated, "she just doesn't do that to anyone unless she knows them.""

F.H.W. Cherry Valley NY

"I used to mow the cemetery and I used to see this elderly man, cane in hand tottering toward the large fenced-in plot of graves in the rear of the graveyard. He would just appear in the middle of the path and totter to the gate and sit down on the step that leads into the graves at that particular plot. I would glance over from time to time and he would be sitting there and then a few minutes later I would look over again and poof, he's gone. Now this did not happen just once but several times. There was no way the man could have walked that fast, no way. He was short and very stooped and had a very slow walk and I would have seen him leave."

B.W.P. Cherry Valley NY

Mr. Roseboom still walks to his grave in the cemetery every day.

"One time I looked up from my mowing and there was this little boy. Near him was this woman obviously watching him. They were dressed in very old-fashioned clothing. I would be mowing near the fountain when I saw them. I would make my round and come back on the next lap of mowing and there they were. Usually three times around and then poof, they're gone, just like that. I even got off the mower once just after one of these incidents and looked all around, but there was no sign of them."

B.W.P. Cherry Valley NY

"My father was a mere teenager and he was driving his mom in their Model T. They were about to go into the cemetery gates and the car stalled and wouldn't start. My father got under the car to see what was wrong when my grandmother demanded that he get the thing started right away. She sounded really anxious and scared. He then heard her say, "Well, will you look at this!" Up the street came a funeral procession. A lady dressed all in white was leading the pack followed by men in tall stovepipe hats and ladies in long black dresses. The hearse was pulled by horses with the coffin plainly visible through the glass in the carriage. They silently went past the car where my very startled and intrigued grandmother sat. The procession turned into the gates of the cemetery and promptly disappeared. The car started right away after that."

R.J.O. Cherry Valley NY

The ghostly hearse in the cemetery.

"There used to be this tall hedge surrounding the cemetery. My grandmother and my mom used to see that *Death Coach*, as she called it quite frequently. My mom, who was a little girl at the time used to go near the hedge looking for it. My grandmother used to admonish her by telling her she would end up like *Alice in Wonderland* and go down the rabbit hole if she wasn't careful."

T.T.S. Webster FL

"I remember my uncle John who used to live next door to the cemetery. He used to walk on the grounds of the cemetery late at night and he used to tell me that he saw all kinds of people and lights and orbs and black and white shadowy figures, it was like a regular party in there. I used to stay with him occasionally and I remember this one day in particular when he burst into the house. He was white as a sheet. I asked him what happened and after he caught his breath he told me he finally saw it. I impatiently asked him what he saw. He said, "the Ghost Coach of course. I finally saw it.""

S.A.R. Roseboom NY

"My father has seen that funeral procession more than once. He used to sit back on the bench near the fountain. The first time he saw it, it scared him to death. Here comes this hearse pulled by horses with men and women following it and they were dressed in eighteenth century clothing. They would go past him as if the funeral was finished and they were going home. As they got to the gates of the cemetery they would just disappear through the hedge and into thin air."

L.J. Cherry Valley NY

The Massacre Monument stands sentinel over the bodies of some of the victims of the Cherry Valley Massacre of 1778.

"Sometimes, near dusk while you are wandering through the cemetery the plaintive sound of a fiddle tune is heard. Faintly, like being carried on a small breeze. It is almost as if it is afraid to be too loud lest it becomes noticeable. Many have heard the ghostly fiddler. No one knows who he is but I can imagine the loneliness of the frontier outposts created the need for a man to indulge his passion for just a little while. The music is haunting, plaintive like a soul forever wandering eternity."

S.M-M. Cherry Valley NY

"I do get this creepy feeling over by the massacre monument. I guess it is just my imagination because when I was just a kid I used to run all around there. I have heard my aunt say that if you look toward the monument on a moonlit night and there is snow on the ground, you can see the ghostly grave diggers burying what was left of the victims of the massacre. I think she used to enjoy scaring me, for as she was telling her story I could just imagine these men in their colonial garb with their shovels in hand. They would turn and stare at me and then slowly, ever so slowly start walking toward me, their bony hands gripping their shovels and their feet silent upon the frozen ground."

J.P.M. Cherry Valley NY

If you are lucky enough to hear the fiddler, the tune is one that you don't forget right away.
It is a haunting tune of great sadness. Just sit and listen for it.

58

"In the cemetery, back in the late 1950's you used to be able to go just inside the gate and there was a stone with an obelisk on top. If you looked at the corner of this stone you could see a large hole and it was a pit. In the pit were many skeletons. They filled in the hole with concrete so no one can see the bodies anymore."

S.W. Gettysburg PA

"When I was a kid that pit was rumored to be the ammunition dump for the old fort. It was where they stored all the powder and balls for the guns and cannon. It was a large room with laid-up stone walls. In the early 1800's, the village placed a large stone slab on the top of it. I guess they could have buried people down in there especially when they needed space for the bodies that were found in the road when they widened it."

G.T. Cherry Valley NY

"I had a really funny experience one time. I played in the school band and we were at the Memorial Day parade. The whole town was there listening to the speeches. I was looking forward to the gun salute, which the American Legion does at the end of the ceremony. I didn't think anything of it at the time but there were these, what I thought were re-enactors all standing there as if at attention. They were just behind the legion men up near the woods at the back of the cemetery. My concentration was averted when we had to get ready to play taps. When I looked back in that direction, they were gone. They were nowhere to be found in the crowd of people either. I mean, there were at least fifteen of them, so they couldn't have disappeared just like that! Impossible."

D.W. Binghamton NY

"Because I could not stop for death,
He kindly stopped for me.
The carriage held but just ourselves,
And immortality."

Emily Dickinson

# French and Indian War Battlefield   East Hill   Morton Road

The first time I heard about someone seeing the ghostly battle I was very skeptical and I buried the idea in the back of my mind. In interviewing people for this book, this particular event surfaced again and it gives me some pause for thought. Now, I know that many of you French and Indian war buffs will pooh-pooh this fanciful tale but who's to know? There were hundreds of unrecorded skirmishes all over this area and we did have an active military and a fort here during that time period; 1754 – 1763. So, who is to say that it couldn't be true; that on some remote hillside two opposing forces ran into one another.

---

"My mother-in-law was very sick and it was our habit to take her out for a car ride on East Hill once a week. It was a pleasant spring morning when she asked us, "Did you see that, did you see that?" We asked her, "See what?" "Why there were men in red coats, other men in blue coats and it looked like some Indians having a fight in that field we just passed." We were bewildered to say the least but she maintained her story until the day she died."
B.H.P.  Cherry Valley NY

"I was cycling past that intersection of road one day and all I could smell was gunpowder and blood. It was awful and I felt sick. I continued my ride past the intersection and it all passed, but the feeling of dread kept with me the entire ride back to Cherry Valley."
T.H.  Cherry Valley NY

"My mother saw something in that field at the intersection many years ago when she was a little girl. She was so frightened that whenever we took that road, which was a shortcut into town she would close her eyes and literally shake. She never told any of us what she saw, including my father, but it must have been really frightening."
E.H.F.  Roseboom NY

"The battle usually occurs at night but there are some who experience it even during the day. Several of my friends have seen it and it scared them to hell. They just shake their heads and say, "I am not going there, I just don't want to discuss it."
R.E.  South Valley NY

"It was gruesome, as all frontier battles were. I mean, when I witnessed it, to me it was like a moment in which I experienced all the carnage of that fight. It was just a moment but I saw it all. I will never forget it. I looked across the intersection into the field going down the hill and I saw men running away and being shot at. I looked in the opposite direction, into the other field and I saw dead men scattered all over it and men bending over bodies like they were taking scalps or robbing bodies. I remember the glint of the copper and silver breastplates of the Indians and the buttons on some of the soldier's uniforms. They were that close. It was as if I was standing in the middle of all of them"

T.S. Milford NY

"I get really creeped out every time I go past the farm and I look down into that valley with the creek running through it. I don't know why but I have strong feelings that people have died there."

F.S. Cherry Valley NY

"My aunt was driving past the farm when all of a sudden she looked across the road and there were soldiers and they were fighting one another. Some were in obvious uniform and others were not, but it was a battle. She almost ran into the ditch."

B.H.P. Cherry Valley NY

"I was biking past that hillside field and I noticed this strong smell of gunpowder and rotting flesh. It was sickening, but it only lasted for a few moments. Then, I passed through this *cold spot* right in the middle of the road. It was like the summer temperature had dropped into the thirties. I glanced to my left and I froze, for there in the field lay all these human bodies. The smoke from the rifles was still hovering around the scene. The whole scene lasted for less than probably thirty seconds. Needless to say, I booked it out of there real fast. Haven't been back there since."

R.F.F. Roseboom NY

# Indian Battlefield      Hoose Road    East Hill

Sometime in the far distant past there was a battle; a battle between several native tribes. Maybe it was for hunting rights or just the normal battle for conquest that went on all through this region from the dawn of time. Native American history can now be traced back in this area to over twenty-thousand years ago and it is interesting to note that there were over three-hundred native languages spoken on this continent at the time of the first European contact. Whenever this battle was it was a brutal battle. It takes place in a large field between two dirt roads on the *State Lands* on East Hill. Several people have seen the battle first hand and the eerie quietness of the place makes one want to look over one's shoulder. You walk down a well-maintained path about half a mile and you come to a slight slope. Once you climb up the slope you are in a large, level field. You feel something, something very menacing and then you observe figures walking toward you, their faces are decorated with war paint and they carry tomahawks and spears.

---

"When we purchased the place, I had all the intentions of planting Christmas trees out there. I have a walking path that I mow frequently. If I walk across that field, which is a good ten acres I reach the old road where it dead ends into a swamp. There have been a few times, while planting trees in the spring that I have these flashbacks. It is like time moving backward and I have witnessed a terrible and bloody battle. Hundreds of Indian warriors are fighting and the next instant I'm witnessing men lying bloody and dead in this field of carnage and then, just before sunset the smell hits you. It's that rotting smell of death. Most of the time I spend less than three hours at a time out there and never after dark. From the relative safety of the deck of our house we have witnessed dancing lights, mists rising from nowhere and heard un-Godly screams from that field. No sir, I don't go out there after dark."

L.M.P.  Cherry Valley NY

"We own the house next door to the people that own the field. Our horses are pastured on the border of that field and not one of those horses will go near that side of the fence. The grass that grows on that side of the pasture is the best grass in the whole place but those horses refuse to go there. One time, while I was mending fence I smelled a foul odor like something had died and was left in the sun to rot. It was an evil odor and it sickened me. It was just a sunset."

S.F.  Cherry Valley NY

"The horses will not go near that field let alone go in it. I've tried riding my mare through there. She will not go into that field, period. One time she even threw me off when I tried to force her into that field."

L.M.  South Valley NY

The Rich – Gilbert cemetery on East Hill is just an example of what you can find while strolling in the woods on a beautiful spring day. Sometimes though, you might have to share the site with others.

# Private Cemeteries

There are many private cemeteries in Cherry Valley. You can find them alongside roads and in fence rows, deep in the woods and sometimes in someone's back yard. They are the vestiges of family plots from times past when life moved at a slower pace.

---

"I was near the Eckerson cemetery when I noticed a little girl standing near the stone wall that surrounds the cemetery. She was only about six or seven. She looked so real. She was just standing by this grave, obviously distraught. She looked at me and this pleading look came over her face and then she disappeared."
E.M.  Roseboom NY

"We were up drinking in the back of the old Flint cemetery. We were sitting there with our beers on this nice night, no wind, not even a breeze. All of a sudden this really cold chill comes across our bodies. Now, there was this tin can that was turned upside down and stuck on one of the fence spikes and that can started to spin. I mean really spin, just like a top; real fast. We didn't know what to think so we hightailed it out of there. Left our beers there! What a waste."

B.Y  Salt Springville NY

"I sometimes see lights up there in the old graveyard at night. They blink and flash as if children are running around with candles. There are a lot of children buried up there, more than usual and I have often wondered just by what hand they could have died. They all range from three months to seven years old and they all died in different years to the same family. Another historian and I were comparing notes and it really makes one wonder."

S.M.  Sharon Springs NY

"One time, late at night as I was driving Route 50 on East Hill I saw this figure of a lady. She seemed rather young and she came across the road in front of me from the cemetery right there at the edge of the road. It looked like she was headed toward the old road that goes into the woods across from the cemetery. I had a feeling she was headed home. There is an old foundation up there. I just wonder."

R.Y.  Roseboom NY

"I have noticed that while walking in the woods, either alone or with someone that when I come across a cemetery or just a small gravesite that I become aware that I might not be alone. I'm not saying that it's the spirit of the person who is buried in that grave. Maybe a family member or acquaintance that's just there for a moment for a visit or just to pay respects or maybe reminisce. I remember one particular time when a group of historians went on a walk to a particular grave yard that was very remote. Within this group on that day were historians and genealogists from four different surrounding towns. We didn't hurry as there was no path to this site and there were older people participating on this walk.
This particular grave yard, although remote was a large site with about fifteen graves. There was a rich carpet of myrtle everywhere and the grass was short as though someone just got finished mowing the lawn. There were spirits everywhere and they were actually having a picnic. I remember one man in particular making a comment about how crowded it was. I looked at him with surprise and he just winked at me."

S.M-M.  Cherry Valley NY

"When I was little and we had a farm, I would always find my little sister up at the old grave site on the hill. She would be sitting there on the ground talking to the air. I asked her one time who in the world she was talking to and she very primly told me it was Grandma she was talking to and that I should mind my own business."

M.J.Y.  Cherry Valley NY

# Time Passes Us All

## The Morse House   Montgomery Street

The Morse House was originally built as a cottage by the Reynolds family in the late 1700's. In early 1800 it was purchased by Jabez Hammond an enterprising attorney in Cherry Valley. Hammond expanded the house and constructed a small law office across the street. Judge James Otis Morse purchased the house and this is where his cousin, Samuel Finlay Breese Morse experimented with the electromagnet for his telegraph machine in 1837.

---

"I grew up visiting the house since I was a little girl and so I had several encounters with both the real person and its spirit. I remember that first time I saw her at the age of six or seven and Cornelia Cox, affectionately known as *Nellie* or *Aunt Nell* was ninety-nine. Nellie lived with her daughter, Cornelia Schwartz, affectionately known as *Aunt Bun* in the Morse House.

Nellie was a little old lady with a stooped posture and she sat in a chair in the garden covered with a heavy shall and a small white dust cap perched on her head. She didn't make much of an impression on me at the time of our first meeting as I was a little kid. Nellie passed from this life in 1945 but that is not the end of the tale.

I encountered her again at the age of eighteen and from then on Nellie made frequent appearances in the Morse House. She would just walk around with her cap on her head and a stooped posture. She never made a sound, just looked around, turned away from the viewer and disappeared. If one did not know she passed on, one would think that it was a person just wearing strange clothing. She did not appear as mist or as white vapor or an orb but as if she had real flesh and blood. It would only be for a few seconds, but there she was. You got used to her and she was not scary at all, she was just there and now someone else has seen her and so I can't be completely looloo."

B.H.  Cherry Valley NY

"My daughter, Meg came to visit my wife and I at the Morse House when she was eighteen. Meg came down stairs the next morning after sleeping in the front bedroom of the house. This bedroom is the one that overlooks the extensive gardens on the property. She casually asked my wife if the house was haunted. My wife, who was preparing breakfast at the time slowly turned to face her and asked her what she saw that would make her ask that question.

Meg said that she was asleep and woke up to the sound of someone opening the door to her bedroom. This little old lady in a high collar dress with a night cap on her head peeked in at her from the doorway. She told us that the lady wasn't frightening, she just looked at her and disappeared. It was almost as if she was doing a bed check."

G.H. Pennsylvania

The Morse House

Back lawn of the Morse House where Aunt Nell liked to sit on summer evenings.

# The Railroad Trestle and Track Bed
## Rte. 166 and Barringer Road

The Cherry Valley Railroad was completed in 1870. It came from Cobleskill through Sharon Springs and ended in Cherry Valley where the engine was turned on a turntable and the train would begin its return trip.

The trains here were not immune to train wrecks and the section between Leesville and Cherry Valley is rather remote but very scenic. The rail service ended here in 1956. The tracks are all gone now but the track bed remains and it has become a favorite walking and cross-country skiing trail.

———————————————

"Just after the dump, as you go in on the old track bed you come to the part where two trestles run parallel to one another. One was unfinished and the other was used by the railroad for many years. It is while you are walking or skiing on that old track bed that you hear the sound of a train. Not the whistle but that rhythmic, clunking sound as the wheels go over the joints in the track; that sound that rocks you to sleep. I have heard it several times in my youth and it gives you a creepy feeling. Do you get out of the way or just stand there in the middle of what was once the track bed."

M.V. Cherry Valley NY

"There was this one time when I was skiing the trestle and I heard the sound of a train. I thought it was really odd so I ignored it. Of course, the sound got louder and louder so I turned around and there, barreling down on me was this vision, for lack of a better word of a very old train locomotive. It was roughly thirty feet from me. This particular spot that I was standing on has a very steep grade and you just don't walk to the side as it is very narrow. Needless to say, I was rooted to the spot and I couldn't even open my mouth for I knew all that would come out of it would be a squeak. Then the train just disappeared, yes just disappeared! I haven't been up on that track bed since."

E.A.M. Rochester NY

Much of the beautiful stone work is still up there on the old track bed.
It is a peaceful place to hike and sometimes you might just see something else.

# Oliver Judd House   Main Street

The house was built in 1804 by Oliver Judd who came here from Connecticut with his wife, Elizabeth and his mother-in-law. He was a blacksmith and ironmaster and started the Judd Iron Foundry in Cherry Valley along with two of his sons. Thirteen children were born in the house and Oliver and his wife died here. This was a Judd house into the late 1940's and it remains a friendly place, full of warmth and cheer because the original inhabitants make sure it stays that way.

------

"Oliver Judd occasionally makes his presence known but he is usually off doing his business. He checks-in if you need him. His son, Dewitt, who drowned in a water trough outside the house makes his presence known especially if there are children or pets about. When our children were growing up it was a virtual nightmare for them as their studies were being constantly disrupted. It seems he was addicted to the game of *Jacks*. In the middle of the night you would hear this quiet thump of a hard rubber ball on the upstairs bedroom floor. He also had the annoying habit of gliding past you and imparting a wisp of breath on your neck or a shadow in your periphery vision. It was at first, unsettling but then comforting knowing they were here. They also love to hide things so we had to address that issue right on."
S.M-M. Cherry Valley NY

"On our porch stood a man I had never seen before. He told me he used to live in our house and then he became very uncomfortable looking, like he had something else to say but he didn't know how to say it. Sensing what I thought he wanted to ask me, I said something to the effect that we were aware of the ghosts here. His eyes lit up and he began shaking his head vigorously. I told him we had been trying for several years to get to know them and them us and in the end, it had worked out. There was never a dull moment and that they were now part of the family.
He told me that he only could bear to stay here for a month. He went on to say that every night his dogs would be locked up in their room and every night someone would let them loose and they would run about the house as if playing with someone. It drove him nuts. He told me he even padlocked the door to their room, but that didn't work either."
E.J.M. Cherry Valley NY

"If Oliver didn't like you he made that known. A close friend of mine always found it difficult to stay the entire night at our house. Toilets would flush in the middle of the night, room lights would blink off and on and the radio would suddenly come to life. This caused my friend an extreme amount of anguish and we would end up escorting her home in the middle of the night."

M.M.M.  Pepperell MA

"Oliver was the protective sort. One afternoon, while minding my store which is in the house, two very unsavory characters showed up. Both quizzed me by asking if I was alone in the house and I lied and told them that I was not. I had my back to the wall and the one started to make his way toward me while the other blocked the doorway. Suddenly all hell broke loose in what was, at that time our living room. One large crash followed by another and then another. The two men looked at one another and headed for the door. They couldn't be gone fast enough.

After regaining my composure and slowing my beating heart to a manageable level I ventured into the living room. There on the floor were the three largest books we owned at the time. Two were from the top shelf of our bookcase but not next to one another and one was from the next shelf down. It was as if an unseen hand pushed one than picked another suitable hefty book and then another and pulled them out of their places on the shelf, letting them fall to the floor."

S.M-M.  Cherry Valley NY

"I was remodeling the pantry a few years ago and I had taken down the shelves, ripped up the floor and was spackling the ceiling. All the while I could feel a pair of eyes at my back, boring into me. They weren't questioning, just hostile like, "What the hell are you doing to my space?" After several days of this uncomfortable feeling I did what my mom said to do and sat down and had a nice talk with the entity we call *Ruthie*. I made it plain that I was just remodeling her space to give it a fresh facelift and to make it look better and to last longer. After about fifteen minutes of this talk I went back to work in an atmosphere that had significantly changed from one of hostility to genuine love and trust. Heck, she even helped me find my misplaced hammer."

S.S.M.  Cherry Valley NY

"One night after dinner my friend Mary, who lived in the Judd House and I went upstairs to bed. I stated very firmly that I didn't believe in ghosts and if there was one here it needed to show itself. The follies of youth! We were having a sleepover and we had the radio on and were enjoying the music when all of a sudden, the radio became very staticky. I went over to move the dial to another channel and the dial moved itself."

J.F.  Brooklyn NY

"I had just had an operation on my hand and I was lying in my bed with a pillow supporting my arm. It was late and suddenly I heard the voice of a small boy with an obvious speech

impediment asking me if I was ok. He told me he didn't want me to die. I was petrified, so I called my mom who came to my bedroom right away. She told me to just tell the boy that I would be ok and that I just had an operation to make my arm better. After I assured the boy that I would be ok there was this sensation on my arm of someone lightly caressing it and a very deep, peaceful feeling came over me. I fell immediately asleep, very contented."
M.M.M. Pepperell MA

"It was my daughter Mary's sixteenth birthday party and all her friends were here celebrating in the backyard. It was getting dark and one of the girls had left her sweater in Mary's room. The girl went to retrieve her sweater and after several minutes there came this bloodcurdling scream from the inside of the house. We all just looked at one another and then Mary, my husband and I and several of the guests said in unison, "the ghost, we forgot to tell her about the ghost" as we ran into the house.
We came upon the body of Mary's friend slumped on the second-floor landing, shaking and pointing to the top of the stairs. She was gasping for breath so we quickly got her outside and began to revive her. One of our sons retrieved the sweater. She told us she had gone up the first set of stairs and turned the corner and it was then that she saw Dewitt at the top of the stairs. He was attired in his knickers, knee socks and high-top shoes and she could see right through him."
S.M-M. Cherry Valley NY

The Oliver Judd Homestead

# Walter Werner House   Cape Wycoff   Co Rte. 54

When Walter died he asked to be cremated. His wife respected his wishes but she had him buried in the swamp out back of the house. He didn't like that for he came back and told her so. Just before his wife died, she had him dug up and gave him a proper burial. He still refuses to leave the house much to the consternation of the current owners who have learned to live with him. He can be very cantankerous. Hammers fly off the counters, keys and tools go missing and his short, bowlegged form is occasionally seen in the bedroom doorway. He loves to have his picture taken and he can be seen in every family picture taken in the house.

"We were clowning around for Halloween and my family took this picture. There is Walter, as usual right in the bottom of the picture. He appears as a mist or a large orb. If he gets real ambitious he appears as he was in real life."
P.B.  Cherry Valley NY

# Oakwood   Rte. 166

Jesse Johnson built his palatial manor house on this spot and promptly sold it to Mathew Campbell of Revolutionary War Fame. It was Matthew and his heirs that constructed the wing and the turrets onto Jesse's manor house and you have what you see today; a house that resembles a castle that is reminiscent of the family castle in Scotland.

---

"I remember the story about a Campbell girl who got pregnant outside of wedlock. The girl was banished from the family. She died in childbirth in the upstairs bedroom and to this day many people hear a child cry."

R.J.  Cherry Valley NY

"I used to see an elderly man on the back porch of the old part of the house. He seemed to be looking over the garden area. He would just stand there in the early evening. I saw him many times as a young woman but not so much now."

S.M-M.  Cherry Valley NY

"The baby crying yes, I remember the crying. It would be three of four abrupt cries and then everything would go silent. I also remember the time we were staying in the cottage just outside the back entrance to the house. Someone or something would always manage to unscrew one of the fuses and we would lose power. We would have to go inside and down into that cellar to put a fuse back in. When it was the winter time we always looked for tracks in the snow, but no tracks. No one was living in the main house at the time."

C.L  Ballston Spa NY

"I remember the stories of a woman running around in high-top sneakers She was a Campbell and this was her favorite mode of dress when not in the public eye."

P.W.  Roseboom NY

"There was a bedroom up on the second floor that really creeped me out. I got chills going into there. I heard the story later that a girl died in that room giving birth to a little baby and no one could stay in that room."

S.W.  Gettysburg PA

Oakwood

# The Lady With the Baby     Doc Ahlers Road

Driving home in a snow storm is unnerving enough, especially with the roads around here. Many are dirt and are hilly and that portends many problems if you aren't careful. That being said, when you see a young woman in a summer dress clutching a baby in her arms and running through the swirling snow at the side of the road, you take notice. Being the Good Samaritan that you are, you slam on the brakes, do a little skidding and sliding and come to a halt. You bolt from your car to pronounce your civic duty "Hey, do you want a ride?" The words are on your lips, but they don't come out. You stand there in the snow and cold in total bewilderment. There is absolutely no one there where there was a woman and a baby just minutes before. You search the ditch, you look in the woods, you glance down the road; nothing.

---

"Oh, the white lady, well me and some of my friends have encountered her over the years. The first time I was about twelve or thirteen years old. We were playing in the woods by the side of my grandfather's house on Doc Ahler's road. We were running around. It was late in the afternoon, about supper time and here comes this lady through the trees. She is dressed all in white but the clothes are very outdated for the 1970's. She had on a lacy dress like you see in a Victorian wedding picture and she is holding a baby. She looks at us and her eyes are sad and pleading. The baby was wrapped in a blanket so you couldn't see its face but I do remember that there was a veil or mist around that baby. Well, one minute she's there floating through the trees and the next minute she's gone. Now, we all saw her so this is not a hallucination. We all freaked, I mean we couldn't get out of the woods fast enough."

S.R.  Cherry valley NY

"Lately, a friend of mine actually got her on a *Critter Cam*. She is there floating in several of the frames, just her torso, no feet or legs and a few frames later she's gone."

S.R.  Roseboom NY

"I have not seen her but I have rescued several drivers who have gone off the road because of her."

G.W.  Cherry Valley NY.

# Through The Veil Of Time

## Sutliff House   Main Street

In the early 1800's, Mrs. Little and her sister lived in a tiny house at the rear of what is today the Limestone Mansion and its brick neighbor, the Sutliff House. Mrs. Little or *Ma Little* as she was locally known, was the aunt of one of our many doctors that practiced in Cherry Valley. She always had herbs drying in the house and she tended her gardens where she grew and processed many types of remedies for healing and invigorating the body. She also frequented the fields and roadsides of Cherry Valley, harvesting flowers and herbs and hauling them to the house to be dried and made into tinctures and salves. Many local folk as well as local doctors used her products. She was reported to be a witch, but in those days even midwives were erroneously called witches.

There is nothing left of the tiny cottage now, but time does have a way of remembering.

---

"With all the things that have happened in this house and all of the people that have lived here, I have nothing to report as far as ghosts go. It's peaceful here and I'm not afraid, but there is one thing that bothers me and I must admit it's strange. My kitchen window looks out into the back yard and every once and a while I'll be doing dishes or cooking and when I glance out the window I'll see this tiny house, like a cabin at the fence line of my back yard. Now, there is nothing there but the overgrown grass and the trees that form the border with my neighbor. I'll blink and the image of the tiny house will be gone. It's happened several times and it seems that I see it on mornings when there's a slight mistiness to the air. Strangest thing."

P.LF.  Cherry Valley NY

# Sunday Morning Worshippers     Wall Street

"I remember just sitting quietly at my upstairs window in the back room of my home, gazing out at Wall Street. It was a cold, snowy morning and it was Sunday. I remember hearing the church bells ringing and all of a sudden down Wall Street came this group of people. What caught my attention was the way in which they were dressed. The boys were in knickers and heavy socks with high-top shoes, the girls were in long dresses with heavy woolen capes and the women, there were several of them were in long black dresses and they were wearing bonnets.

There were no leaves on the trees, so my view was unobstructed. They were obviously going to church, but in which time period and where? I remember rushing downstairs and out the front door in my bare feet and with no jacket or sweater. I now could get a good look at them as they rounded the corner of Wall Street and proceeded onto Main Street, or so I thought; but nothing, absolutely nothing. They had just vanished into thin air. One minute I saw them and the next they were gone."

P.L.  Cherry Valley NY

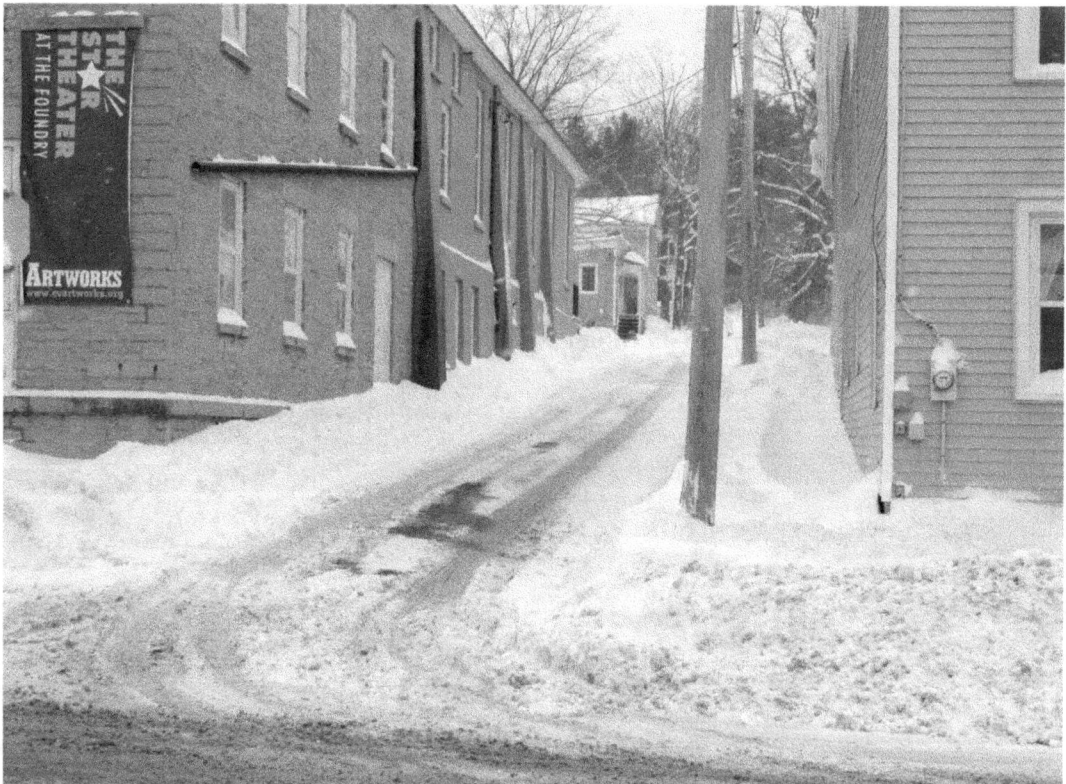

Looking up Wall Street in Cherry Valley

# Used Car   Main Street

"Beep, beep, beep, the incessant honk of a car horn woke me up from my sound sleep. The noise was coming from our driveway and what would the neighbors think at this hour of the morning? It can't be that someone was trying to steal our new, used car could it? It was a classy car, white with dark blue velvet interior and a black top. Two doors, large back seat. We had bought it from a dealer near Schoharie and the price was right; cheap. It had plenty of class even for the most discerning of teenage girls and their friends. It seems that fate had some ideas of its own.

One of our teenage daughters and her friends drove it to Albany one evening and by the time my daughter got home no one wanted any part of the vehicle. Her friends who were sitting in the back seat claimed that it felt like someone or something wanted to sit in each of their laps on the ride down and that they kept getting slapped and pinched by tiny hands. Several months later both my girls had to do last minute Christmas shopping in Albany, fifty miles away. They made it thirty-five miles when they frantically called us to pick them up as the car wanted to drive itself and enough was enough.

Now this was before *Car Fax,* therefore when buying a car all you had to go on was the dealer or seller's honesty when they sold you the car. We were really bewildered by the whole thing.

In servicing the car after this incident, our mechanic found nothing mechanically wrong with the automobile but for one exception, the vin numbers on the door and the vin numbers on the windshield did not match up. Our mechanic proclaimed that the car had been in an accident. After much investigation the mystery was finally solved. The car was indeed in an accident and two little boys were killed in the back seat of that automobile."

S.M-M.  Cherry Valley NY

# Encounters with "Jackie Foster"   Co. Rte. 50

Jackie Foster was a rare individual. He participated in the Battle of Culloden, known as the "45" in Scotland on the side of the British, coming to the colonies shortly after. He was a particular friend of Joseph Brant and as a Tory and devout Loyalist, he acted as a spy for the British in the early days of the American Revolution. Drunk, loud and raucous Jackie homesteaded near to the Hugh Mitchell place just off County Route 50. Hugh tolerated him for the most part and to most folks around here, Jackie was the local *character*, the stuff legends were made of. Jackie could out run the fastest, out lie, out steal, out cheat and out drink anyone that came into his company and was known to regularly trade his women for liquor.

Although most people at that time did not go into his personal life, he still remained the supreme subject of gossip among the women of the settlement.

But, even loyalist sympathizers couldn't save themselves on that day in November. Jackie lost everything he labored for in this new world and then some when the Seneca and the Tories came calling. He was lucky to be able to outrun them.

Like many of our settlers, he did return in 1786, settled down some and became a devout husband and devoted father and lived to be one-hundred years old. And all the while he kept up his banter and lewdness and pitted one judge in this settlement against another judge in the next settlement. Life around Jackie was an ever-ending drama and he liked it that way. Jackie still prefers the woods and the fields and to this day one can still encounter him along the stream called Brimstone Creek.

# Tekeharara Falls "Place of High Waters" Rte. 166 and US 20

Water from natural springs deep below the earth's surface form a small pond near the top of the ravine close to the exit of US Rte. 20 at Cherry Valley. At the top of the ravine the water cascades over the edge forming the one-hundred-eighty-foot high Tekeharara Falls. Sometimes on moonlit nights, if you happen to be on the trail that leads to the bottom of the gorge you can hear faint sounds of rattles and chanting. It is here also that you sometimes catch a glimpse of a tall Indian in full regalia on the cliffs. He stands silently, just watching and waiting. Even at the time of the initial settling of our town in the 1740's, the legend of

the Indian persisted. This has been a solitary place for hundreds of years as it was here that Native American Shamans performed their ceremonies, mixed their healing medicines and ministered to the sick and the dying of their communities. Indian gardens grew naturally at the foot of the first switchback on the path into the gorge. Today, unless you know what species of plants you are looking for, they remain invisible. But, if you know what you are looking for there is a plethora of native medicinal plants here, attesting to the self-reliance of the native healers. This area is filled with caves and this particular cave was very large. It was reached from the base of the falls, the opening being plainly visible from the stream bed. The cave reached back for several miles and branched out in several directions and many old timers have said it was down-right creepy inside. Old hides, drum beaters, wooden tubs and baskets, beads and animal bones littered the floor of the cave. From the 1930's on it was beer bottles that comprised most of the litter in

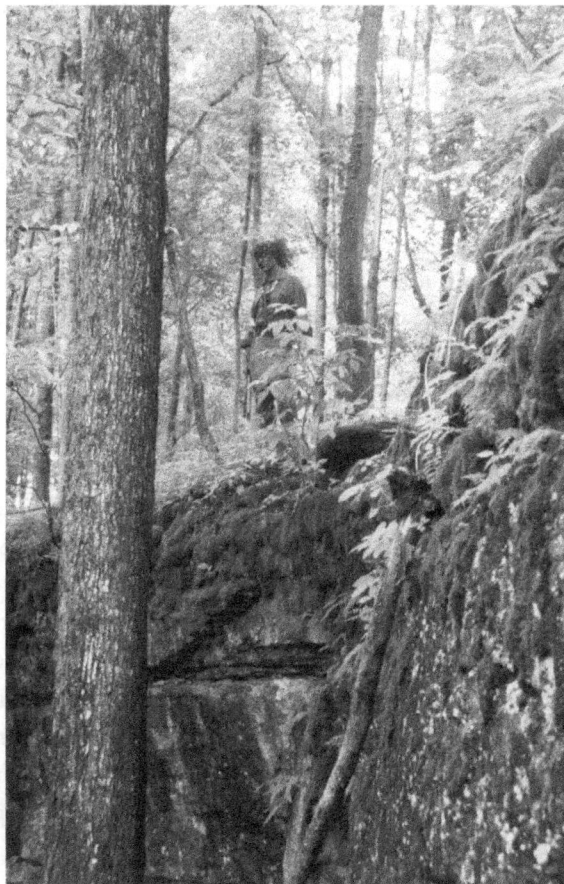

the cave. Then, in 1950 along came the bulldozers and the blasting equipment to create a new road through the area called the *Cherry Valley Bypass*. With the blasting came the demise of the cave and its entryway was sealed forever. But, when the light is right you can still see the figure of the lone Indian on the cliff near the falls, silently watching and waiting.

# Pickerd/Jerdon (Yerdon) Homestead     East Hill

In the woods is a homestead and like many of its abandoned ilk all that is left is a few stone walls, the foundation and if you look hard enough, the remains of an old graveyard.

---

"We came upon it unexpectedly while following a line of cairns into the woods. We were hoping to find more cairns, but we ended up with more than we bargained for. We noticed the stone walls first and then the cellar hole. Looking past this to my right I spotted an area enclosed in what was once a stone wall. The stones were scattered about like leaves blown in a wind storm. I peeked into the center and there, in neat rows were six depressions in the ground. They were maybe three feet by five feet with one being smaller than the rest.
My walking partner for this excursion was Nancy, a long-time friend and psychic who was visiting for the day. Nancy came up behind me and stated, "Who's the girl?" I looked up from the graves and faintly I could see her in the late afternoon shafts of sunlight. She was a pretty little girl with long, white-blonde hair. She wanted to play. Suddenly, the air turned very cold and a voice, high and raspy stated very firmly, "What do you want? Get away."
Nancy and I were startled. We both began to think thoughts and receive thoughts about this little wizened woman. She was protecting *her child.* I got the firm impression that she was the grandmother and the child just refused to go on into the *light.* She wanted to stay here and play.
Nancy and I gave each other knowing glances and started talking to the little girl. We addressed her carefully. The name Sarah came to mind several minutes into our dialogue. We told her that there was a place much more wonderful than this place where she was at the moment and she could easily go to it if she wanted to.
Nancy sat on a rock that jutted out from one of the stone walls and I sat on the ground in a pile of leaves. We relaxed, this was going to be good as we were both in tune with her and her grandmother. "There will be all kinds of little girls and boys there to play with and all kinds of toys and it is warm and beautiful there all the time," I said. "Yes, that is true," said Nancy, "and your grandmother and you will be together as well as your mom and dad and many other people you knew in this place long ago." Sarah asked us how and we told her to take her grandmothers hand, go toward the light and walk into it. "God will show you the way," said Nancy.
Suddenly, we noticed that it was getting very dark. The sun was setting rapidly. We no longer noticed the coldness that surrounded us a few moments ago. They were gone. We each said a silent prayer of farewell, stood and blessed the area.
"Can we get out of here?" said Nancy with a lot of concern in her voice. "Yes, we just have

to go straight back the way we came and make sure to keep the fading sun light at our right shoulders," I said. We managed to do some tripping and stumbling through the underbrush and finally I could see the road below us and my vehicle. "Be careful, this is one heck of a hill in the dark," I said as we bumbled our way to the hard surface of the road.

I hope that it's peaceful there now and that two very nice souls have found their way home."

S.M-M. Cherry Valley NY

# Dutcher House   Boyd Place     Morton Road

This was once a palatial home perched on top of a high hill in the middle of remote wilderness. The home was filled with family when constructed in the 1830's on land once owned by the Spencer Clan at the bottom of the hill. This was the home of the fourth son of Ruloff Dutcher, Marquis Dutcher. Ruloff resided on the main road just two miles from this house. Dutcher houses sprang up all around this area. Many stand today, testimonials to a productive and enterprising family. Then, as always, the family disintegrated and others bought the property.

Known as the Boyd House in the 1960's it was abandoned except for occasional family visits. In the 1970's, kids partied in the house and it was the scene of purported satanic rites at night and all of this managed to color the house as haunted.

Whatever was in there first, before the 1940's was friendly but subsequent sessions with Ouija boards and satanic rites managed to introduce a new layer into the scene. The house became malevolent and forbidding, even when visited in daylight it watched you.

You approach the house from a muddy, not so trodden path. Weeds trip you and blackberry bushes nick your legs as you breathlessly climb the rise to where the house sits surveying its domain. You can spot it, a roof peeking out from a canopy of maples and shadblow, but you have to know where to look. In the summer, it hides its face but, in the winter, when the leaves fall its roof peak faces the sky like a sunbather inviting warm rays onto its beseeched face.

The canopy of trees that surround the place give it an eerie feeling of closeness. Windows, long devoid of glass, defaced walls and stairs leading to nowhere and debris dot its interior. Of the most distracting is the lintel over the main doorway. It is strange, for maybe it is a bit too fancy for the remoteness of the place. You notice that a circular drive once graced the front of the house and there were neat beds of flowers that grew along the abandoned brick walkway.

You become aware of distant singing; the high plaintive voice of a small boy. Happy thoughts fill your mind. Who was this boy who lived here many, many years ago? Why is he so lonesome, so afraid? Into your mind swoops another image, that of an old man. He is demanding that you leave. He wants you gone and the sooner the better. The house is his and all that surrounds it is his. But the evil feelings that envelop you now do not belong to this pair, but to something else, something that had arrived with others, years after the earth had silenced the old man and the boy. There are layers here, layers of time. Each wanting to be dominant, each fighting for the right to tell a story.

This place is an enigma, where time stands still and the dead make their way among the ruins of a once grand and noble home.

Leaving, you almost run to get away from the heaviness of the air surrounding the area. The house seems to say, "go, go…let me be in peace." It's not the company of the living that it hungers for but the company of the dead.

We made our way back to the house ten years later and there definitely was a change in the atmosphere. Things are at peace now. Gone were most of the walls of the house and the barn had collapsed into the ground where moss and grass now find a foothold.

The boy and the man are gone now also. No more singing, no more "go away." It seems that they, as well as the house have made peace with time.

---

"I remember the noise, like someone shouting at us and the feeling of dread as we went up there that summer afternoon. I have never felt anything like that before and never after it."
M.M. Mobile AL

"There was always this story that a young woman died there on her wedding night"
J.F. Brooklyn NY

"Boyd House, yes I remember it well from my childhood. I used to cut through the woods to get there as it always intrigued me. The closer I got to that house the more screaming I would hear, as if there was a woman in mortal distress."
T.S. Cherry Valley NY

"I remember the uncomfortable feeling of the place, the blood splatter on the walls, painted red pentagrams and the 666 spray painted on the exposed lath. That really creeped me out. I remember the feeling that Sue was having about the man and the little boy of about five years old. I remember when we were walking away from the house and going down the path, I heard singing. Yes, very definitely singing. Several years later I went up there with some friends and stumbled upon a gravestone. It was the grave of a little boy. I remember vividly what Sue had said about a little boy and an old man being there."
J.F. Brooklyn NY

The decorative lintel over the doorway of the Dutcher – Boyd House.

"I hunted up there for years. Creepiest damn place I've ever been to. I swear that place just sat there and watched you."
L.H. Cherry Valley N

# Cherry Valley Old School and Community Center
## Genesee Street

The Old School building was built in 1913 on land donated by Mrs. Sarah Waldron. A new school building was built when our school system merged. Today the building is used as a community center with the village and town offices occupying some of the space along with a day care, spa and exercise area and our post office.

---

"It was over fourteen years ago. I was about sixteen years old and one afternoon some friends and I snuck into the old school. The building was stripped as the school had recently moved to its new location further up the road. The place was a mess. We were standing up on the balcony overlooking the gym. Suddenly, I spied the figure of a man coming through the doors below us. This was a figure you could look right through but you still could see it was a person. We hightailed it out of there as fast as we could, but when we got down to the first floor he was right there in front of us but going in the opposite direction down the hallway. We really lost it when he went gliding right through the wall at the opposite end of the hall."

D.J.C. Cherry Valley NY

"Two of my friends are Girl Scouts and they meet at the Old School in the gym. My two friends had stayed behind to help turn off the lights and pick up. Both of them were near the stage and all but one of the lights was off when my friend, Sarah noticed a man sitting quietly up in the second floor balcony overlooking the gym. She shouted at him to leave as they had to lock up. My other friend bounded across the gym into the hallway and up the stairs to the second floor balcony. There was no one there. She turned around and went down the stairs and noticed that Sarah was standing in front of the doorway leading to the stairs that go to the upstairs balcony. She was staring at something down the hallway. She joined her just in time to see the figure of a man go right through the wall."

Z.S. Cherry Valley NY

"I was measuring the gym for an event we were having and was just finishing up the task. Our town clerk entered the gym and started turning off the lights. I started down one hallway as I was going to go out another door at the opposite end of the building. I approached the intersection of the two hallways and suddenly this black figure just walked in front of me like a flash. He entered the hallway where the stairway was to the second floor balcony. He went right through the wall and disappeared."

S.M-M. Cherry Valley NY

"There is a place in the Old School where there are several steps leading up to a small office. It is the old projector room and there are tons of activity in that space. Little children like to play *cat and mouse* with you."

L.M.  South Valley NY

"Last night's sleep-over in the gym with the Girl Scouts was interesting. I woke up and it was pitch black and about three in the morning. There was this outline of a man standing in the doorway. It seemed to me he was just checking up on us, that's all. Needless to say, I did not venture out to go the bathroom as I had intended to do."

D.W.  South Valley NY

"I always smell Mr. Lindsay's cigarettes in the old athletic office whenever I'm near that area and I'm always hearing doors slamming when I'm in there during the day. It's as if school is still in session."

D.W.  South Valley NY

"I still think one of the spirits down there is the custodian. Everyone called him Dewey. He took care of the place for many years. He was a really nice guy."

F.R.  Cherry Valley NY

"I just don't like going in there, the place makes me feel uncomfortable. No matter what the function is, I feel like I'm still at school or at least classes and activities are still going on around me. Yes, I'm that sensitive to it. I went to the psychic fair in there the other day and even the psychics were commenting on all the spirit activity."

J.G.  Cherry Valley NY

# Spook Hollow   Co Rte. 50

Lots of unexplained things happen in Spook Hollow. Now according to one local, Spook hollow is at the near end of Wilson Road where it used to come into Co. Rte. 50 on the corner near the old Spencer farm. That end of the road is now un-passable but you can still come in from the other end.

This is where, when the moon is full it is reported that feral cats will talk to passersby in high-pitched voices, owls swoop low overhead, strange balls of light are seen on the horizon, mists suddenly surround you and you find yourself in the midst of an army of men in military uniforms marching; but to where? And this is also where, according to local legend, skeletal horses and riders race down the road at breakneck speed as if racing the devil himself.

---

"I remember my father telling me this story. One day a peddler and his helper were traveling from Center Valley to Cherry Valley. Now, at that time Wilson Road was the shortest way between the two places and everyone took that route. His team of horses got to the bottom of the hollow and there they stayed. No matter how hard they pulled they could not budge the wagon. The brake was off, no mud or ruts obstructed the road and the wheels were all good. The peddler who knew the reputation of the road told the helper to "hold and wait," as it was nearing midnight. At exactly midnight this ball of light appeared on the horizon in the road. Swiftly it approached the team and the two men. The ball of light bore down on the little party in the road and passed right between the legs of the horses and the four wheels of the wagon and disappeared. The peddler immediately took up his place on the seat of the wagon and proceeded the rest of the way to Cherry Valley without incident."

J.J. Cherry Valley NY

"Many times, over the years couples going home that way late at night from a movie at the movie theatre on Main Street would encounter strange things. Even on hot summer nights you never rolled down the windows in your car as you were passing through the dip just before the corner of Rte. 50 and Morton Road. Invariably, cars would lose power on this road and no matter what one did, the car would not start. Many people became stranded here until sunup but no way would they get out of the car."

R.J.O. Cherry Valley NY

"Myra McFee Johnson's brother used to deliver the mail up into Spook Hollow and Center Valley in the early 1900's. Going through Spook hollow was the shortcut into Cherry Valley in those days. He used to tell us strange stories he heard of things that happened up in there after dark and the rule of thumb was you get out of there at sunset if not before."

L.J. Cherry Valley NY

"When I was younger my relatives used to tell me of the spring up on Morton Road. This spring had the best water around and there was an old wooden sign there that had hand painted letters that just said *Water*. Many people stopped and filled their buckets and jugs with the water from this spring. There was an old house that stood by the spring but even in the 1950's that house was gone. Some said it was a witch that lived there, others say an old man and woman but either way, the place scared me. I could imagine all sorts of goings on. I think I was reading too much Hansel and Gretel. Anyway, that is what I thought of the site; straight out of a fairy tale book with the boy and girl, the witch and the gingerbread house."

R.J.O. Cherry Valley NY

"My grandmother used to scare us with tails of this spring at the side of the road up in the very center of Spook Hollow. She told me they called it *Witches Hole* and if you drank the water from that spring you would have magical powers. Needless to say, I tried to get there as much as possible to drink the water, especially before a major test at school."

L.J. Cherry Valley NY

The spring, center of the picture flows into the small creek and then under Morton Road and down into the valley below.

# McClung Mansion  Limekiln  Alden Street

Built on the grounds of the old Ritchie Farm from Revolutionary War days, the mansion was constructed by Pittsburg Pennsylvania industrialist, Alfred McClung as a summer residence for his wife, Mary Melon McClung in 1920. Built in the style of Colonial Revival Architecture, the mansion was modeled after Willow Hill, which stands at the top of the hill on Fish and Game Club Road, less than a mile from this house.

Limekiln was named for the many lime kilns that once flourished on the property. The fireplace mantles in the house are the remains of the mantles from homes that were torn down in Cherry Valley, or so the story goes.

Many parties and lots of family used the home in the early days and there is a story about a caretaker, a Mr. VanDewerker who shot himself at the end of the driveway one evening in the 1920's. In the 1940's, the home was turned into a hotel for several years. In 1988 the Glimmerglass Opera acquired the home. The house is currently used as quarters for opera singers during the summer opera season of the Glimmerglass Opera.

Mary Melon-McClung quietly watches guests come and go from the top of the stairs at Limekiln.

Alfred McClung's summer house The Limekiln.

"The new kitchen is very nice but there is someone there and they aren't too pleased that I'm in their space. It could be a servant or cook trying to figure out just how many guests will be to dinner. I don't know, but they are not happy I am visiting."

M.M. Pepperell MA

"There is always someone behind me, watching me as I go about my work here. The feeling can be very oppressing at times especially in the *servant's quarters*. There is one door you can't keep closed and the lady at the top of the stairs is seen frequently. The house is very *busy*. It is almost like they are going about their business and I'm going about my business but never the two shall meet."

L.M. South Valley NY

"Many years ago, before the opera purchased the property in the 1980's, we lived in a house that bordered the property. The kids used to go over there and look at the house as they were intrigued by the large tennis court that was there at the time. My daughter and a friend of hers have seen ghostly games of tennis being played on that old tennis court that has since been torn down. The remains of the limestone quarry are just down a path from the house and several times my son and his friends have had encounters with a ghostly man with a pickax. The remains of the Ritchie Farm foundation are still evident on the back lawn. They tried to burn the house down on the day of the massacre in 1778, after capturing Mr. Ritchie but because the house was made of stone, only the inside was damaged. As I said before there are lots of layers of souls there all living out their lives."

S.M-M. Cherry Valley

Throw a party and all the relatives show up…all of them. Just look out the window!

# Bitter Memories

## Ferguson Cellar Hole      Fish and Game Road    Clyde Gulf

The grass waves lazily as Ed, Dan and I make our way past the remnants of a long ago home and barn. The field is mowed now and the hay is harvested and as we approach our destination we are aware of the absence of all sound. It's as if we have entered a vacuum. As we quietly stand at the edge of the hole we notice that the piled rocks make a neat wall below the ground. Most of the hole though, is hidden beneath tangled boughs and matted grass. This is a small place, the remains of a tiny cabin in the wilderness where a family could make a new beginning or so it was hoped.

This is the Ferguson cellar hole. A deadly place in the annuals of Cherry Valley history. It was here that Mrs. Ferguson and one of her children met their end in a horrible act of vengeance. She held onto her baby on that fateful day, as she was punched and beaten. The child was finally loosed from her clutches only to be brutally murdered before her eyes. It was then the attackers spotted her rings; antique rings that could fetch a fortune on the frontier or better yet, be bartered for whiskey. Jane Ferguson glanced down at her hands for she knew what was coming. No matter how hard she tried she could not remove her rings. A swift blow to the back of her head ended the matter. She never felt or saw her demise coming but she sensed it. Her fingers were removed one by one to extract the rings from her death grip.

A family lay shattered that day. The victims were never buried, just left to lie on the frozen ground in the sleet and the snow of a November day in 1778. The bodies were never recovered but the story lives on for there were witnesses to the event. Years later it would be retold in terrifying detail of what really happened that fateful day at the *cellar hole.*

---

"I grew to be an adult on that lonely farm beside the beaver pond. I played at the edge of the swamp in the fields in the summer. It was always windy there and the grass always swayed and made that swishing noise when it moved in the breeze. I remember my sister and I asking my father about that hole beside the field and why he just didn't fill it in. My father called it the *ol' cellar hole.* He told us that long ago there was a family lived there but along came the Indians and the British during the Cherry Valley Massacre and the family was all wiped out. That is all he would tell us but I don't think he knew any more either.

One day, as I lay in the tall grass near to that spot I realized that there was an absence of all sound. No birds chirping, no whir of the locust and no sounds from the crickets and other insects that buzzed around. There wasn't even the sound of the wind. I remember to this day lying there in the grass and thinking of the Nancy Drew mystery series I was reading. I thought, was this what was meant by *deathly quiet?*"

E.G. Ann Arbor MI

"I remember my father saying that when he was little he used to have the job of mowing that field of hay. His mother was always apprehensive until she heard the tractor coming up the road to their house and she knew he was ok. He always had the impression that something happened there in that field, many years ago but no one would talk about it. It was a feeling, a knowing so to speak and he always respected that.

One day he ran out of gas near the edge of the field and as he jumped off the tractor he heard this strange sound. When he finally figured it out, it sounded like someone crying. He went over to the edge of the field and there was, what seemed to be a hole in the ground with laid-up stone for walls. An overwhelming feeling of sadness overcame him. He wasn't frightened, just intrigued but he never told his parents about the experience."

J.J. Cherry Valley NY

Jane Ferguson still weeps for her dead babies in the field near the cellar hole.

# The Hugh Mitchell Place     Co Rte. 50

The dammed up water from the reservoir falls noisily to the base of the falls where it continues on its meandering way to the Cherry Valley Creek, three miles away. On the bank of this stream stood the business establishment of Hugh Mitchell and his family. They ran a saw mill and lived in a small cabin on the property, until that fateful day of November 11th, 1778 when his wife and four of his children were murdered during the Cherry Valley Massacre. The next day, Hugh Mitchell took his gristly cargo, loaded them on a sleigh and slogged through ice and snow to make his way to the fort and safety.

---

"I was on a mission and that was to find the Hugh Mitchell homestead. I was with his great, great granddaughter and we were two determined females. We were being scratched by raspberry bushes, tripped by vines and bit by insects as we steadily made our way through the soggy ground toward the spot. There it was, a hole now reduced to a small depression in the earth. There was once a cabin with a porch and fireplace here on this spot. We were elated and sat and ate our lunches and relaxed and talked about the stories of Hugh Mitchell and his experiences on the Cherry Valley frontier. The legend goes that sometimes on still evenings in the late fall, when the snow blankets the ground, the moon is full and the shadows are deep, shrill, plaintive wails of distress are heard from this small hollow. If you turn and go to the top of the hill overlooking the village, there below you in the field you can sometimes glimpse the lone figure of a man heading in the direction of the village and what was once the fort. He is pulling a sleigh through the snow and stillness of the night."

S.M-M. Cherry Valley NY

Wormuth's horse still races along the dirt road into Cherry Valley

Wormuth Rock

# Wormuth Rock    VanDewerker Road

When you walk Butler Road at night, sometimes there is an uncanny feeling of dread as you approach the old lime kiln. On this section of the road, on some moonlit nights one can hear the beating of horses' hooves on the hard packed earth. The sounds of hoofbeats come closer and closer and in a flash, they are gone. If you are privileged enough to glimpse the horse, you will see a frightened, sweat streaked animal with a blood soaked saddle. This apparition is the rider-less horse of Lt. Matthew Wormuth, returning to Fart Alden after his master was brutally murdered by a friend who mistook him for a foe.

As you walk further you will turn abruptly into the eastbound ramp of US Rte. 20 and what we locals call the *bypass*. At this point you have to cross under US 20 off of Rte. 166 and then get back on it at VanDewerker Road. This was the original road into Cherry Valley and went down into Sprout Brook or Bowman's Creek, as it was known in the old days, and then on to Fort Plain and the Mohawk Valley.

As you continue on VanDewerker Road, just past the intersection of Salt Springville Road on the left you will see a large rock called Wormuth Rock. The time frame is the American Revolution and the date is early May 1778. A young lieutenant from Palatine Bridge, Matthew Wormuth and a neighbor, Peter Seitz are returning to the Mohawk Valley from the Fort at Cherry Valley. Little known to them, native American warrior and British Commander, Joseph Brant and some of his men were waiting in ambush behind the rock in the dense shade of the trees surrounding it.

As the two riders approached the rock the British and Indians fired upon the two men, mortally wounding Wormuth and killing Seitz's horse. Seitz was captured and Wormuth, who they couldn't save was scalped and left in the road. Joseph Brant realized too late that the man he fired upon and killed was a good friend and his neighbor. Even today, you can sit and contemplate the nearby woods and sometimes on the wind there are sounds that come to the ears of this violent, deadly struggle that had imprinted itself on this place.

---

"My mom and I used to walk that road at night. It was on those quiet, moonlit nights that I remember most vividly. She used to tease me about the horse that could almost run you over on the road if you weren't careful. I myself never encountered the spook horse but several friends of mine have."

L.M.  South Valley NY

"Every time I bike past that rock, I get the feeling that someone's watching me. It's really creepy because the feeling isn't friendly at all."
S.T.  Milford NY

"My kids used to play in that field where the rock is. Something happened one day that my kids won't talk about and they won't go near the rock anymore either."
D.L.L.  Cherry Valley NY

"Conscience is no more than the
dead speaking to us."

Jim Carroll

# Putt's Rock    White Lake NY

Putt's Rock is a rose granite spire that reaches several hundred feet into the air. It is next to a limestone cliff in a quarry in the small community of White Lake NY. What has this got to do with Cherry Valley you may ask? Well, let me tell you the story of that rock and what is buried beneath it.

No one had heard of the tale until an historian in the Town of Long Lake actually found it written down in the diary of one of the Durant girls of Blue Mountain Lake. Through the years it has been both an enigma and a mystery as to the truth or falsity of the story. It seems that a Private Putnam was in the ranks of the regular militia under the command of Colonel Klock. On November 11, 1778, Klock's forces marched to the aid of Colonel Alden's forces during the Cherry Valley Massacre. They arrived a day later and too late to assist in anything else but burying the dead. Putnam's fiancé was one of the casualties of the attack and he vowed revenge. Taking seven men with him, they set out in pursuit of the men that murdered his beloved.

Finding out that small parties of the main attacking force of the Tories, British and Indians had split off from the main force under the command of Walter Butler, they pursued the individuals who they felt were responsible for the atrocities. Instead of heading west toward the Finger Lakes and on to Fort Niagara as the main force of attackers under Walter Butler had done, they headed north and into the Adirondacks.

At the hamlet of White Lake, the pursued waited in ambush for Putnam and his men. It was not a long wait. All eight of the men, including Putnam were murdered and scalped at the base of the rock. Their mutilated bodies were covered with leaf mold and left. They are rumored to be there today, for on certain quiet November evenings lights appear at the base of the rock and muffled cries can be heard over the sound of the wind.

---

"I have lived here in White Lake all my life. My father used to tell me that if I played in the quarry after dark he would see me real soon after with my "tail between my legs." When I was in high school a group of friends wanted to go out one night, so I snuck out to join them We headed for the quarry with beer and cigarettes and selected a nice flat spot at the foot of the big granite spire that rose into the air from the quarry wall several hundred yards in from the entrance. We spread out our blankets and began our party. We talked and drank and smoked for maybe about an hour when I noticed the boy across from me looking over my shoulder with this look of terror on his face. His hair was standing straight up and his eyes looked glazed over, like he was going to faint. I felt goosebumps all over me. The girl next to me looked around and screamed. That scream echoed off the walls of that quarry and even today, seventy years later I can still hear them. She told me later that there were several men standing behind me and that they looked like skeletons and that they were dressed in rags and were covered in what seemed to be blood. I came home that night with my "tail between my legs.""

E.M. White Lake NY


"My uncle worked in that quarry for many years and he always made sure he was home before dark. He drove the loader and filled the dump trucks with stone. He told me there were things that he couldn't explain going on in that quarry. That's all he would say."

D.M. Lake Placid NY

Top of Putt's Rock in White Lake N.Y.

# Spy Ridge    State Rte. 166

Just south of Cherry Valley is a ridge that runs parallel to Route 166. On this ridge one could keep tabs on the comings and the goings of the people of the Valley. Just below the ridge is an old Indian trail that was actively used during the Revolution and especially the days that preceded the massacre.

---

"I remember hiking on that ridge and stopping to sit and relax at the spot where the rocks form a platform and there are no trees growing there. It was one of my favorite vantage points as you can see the entire village below. Several times, as I made my way up the steep slope and crossed the old Indian trail I could see men standing on top of that knoll just above me at my favorite spot. When I finally got to the top to see who they were, no one would be there. This happened several times and I casually told my uncle what I saw. He told me that was the place that Colonel Walter Butler and some of his scouts spied on the fort the day before the massacre."

G.H. Binghamton NY

"One day, several years ago several friends of mine and I decided to go for a hike. We started at Porth Road and cut across the ridge past the powerlines and toward the village keeping to an old Indian trail through the woods. All of a sudden there is this force that hit me right in the middle of the back, like something just ran into me. I staggered and fell off the path and started rolling down the slope. I caught myself just in time. I was badly shaken but we proceeded along the path and suddenly we couldn't go any further as the path ended at a steep slope that was very rocky. This time it was my friend that was pushed from behind. I saw his body jerk forward and then he's falling and there is nothing any of us could do. We scrambled down the slope after him and ended up in a farmers plowed field. The thing that really creeped me out was the sound of laughter. Someone was laughing at us. It was a deep laugh that was very creepy, but no one was around."

C.Y. Cooperstown NY

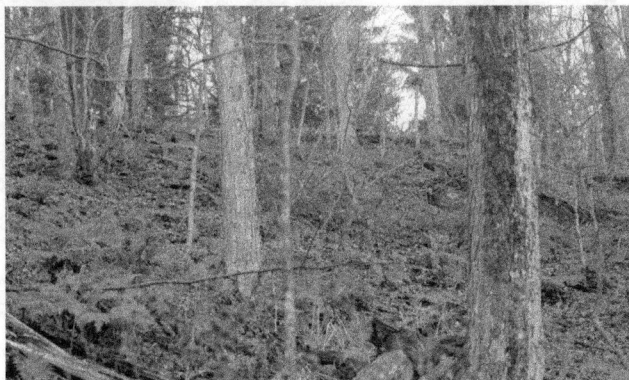

Looking up at Spy Ridge from the old Indian trail. Sometimes you can see men standing on the rocks at the top, but who are they?

# Duplop Monument    Genesee Street

A lot happened here on this small plot of land where Rev. Samuel Dunlop and his wife made their home. Rev. Dunlop shaped this small community into a place of independent spirit with an ethic for hard work. These were the plans of an educated Scots-Irish preacher and his strong-willed wife for their community of independent thinkers in Cherry Valley. On the morning of the massacre of 1778, Rev Dunlop was an elderly man. His wife by his side, he witnessed her brutal murder and di-section, a scene he never recovered from. Now, many years later the essence of that brutal day still pervades the spot where the incident happened. Time and place never forget.

---

"My mom used to say that if you sit quietly near the Dunlop Monument, site of the cabin of Rev. Samuel Dunlop, you hear things. Sometimes it is only a whisper and other times it's crying and weeping, and the smells of wood smoke and the iron smell of blood."
L.M.  South Valley NY

The Dunlop marker, site of Rev. Samuel Dunlop's cabin.

"We are so afraid of the idea of having
to die...that we always try to find excuses
for the dead, as if we were asking beforehand
to be excused when it is our turn."

Jose' Saramago

# Life On The Other Side

## Clark Farm  Co Rte. 50

The place was originally the farm of George Clark in the 1850's and then it passed into Steenburgh hands and from there became the property of John Gedart. In the glen across the street was the original Armstrong Saw Mill. The mill moved to the edge of town in the mid 1800's and became the Armstrong Chair Factory.

The town road ran along the side of the house on the south side. It is abandoned as a road now but is still used as a driveway to reach the rear of the house. The barns across the street are vestiges of what they once were and the old milk house had collapsed with the snows of last year. There are still remnants of the old orchard and on summer nights just before sunset there is a quiet peace about the place. It is a happy place and if you walk the fields down to the old creek bed the remains of the old saw mill can still be seen. If you follow the stream toward town, which is the Cherry Valley Creek you will come to Livingston's Falls and the old swimming hole.

---

"We were traveling home to Cherry Valley when we passed the old farm. It was New Year's Eve and me and my sister and two brothers were in the car. It was lightly snowing and all of a sudden there was a little girl of about two to three years old in an old fashioned sleigh at the top of the snow bank in front of the driveway to the barns.
My sister asked, "did you see that?" The three of us nodded yes. We quickly turned around and went back, but there was nothing there not even tracks in the snow."
R.J.O.  Cherry Valley NY

"As we approached the driveway to the barn I saw a small girl of about two years old sitting in an old fashioned sleigh, the kind of sleigh that was more of a box with runners. She was sitting on top of the snow bank in the sleigh at the side of the road. The little girl was obviously having fun as she was waving her arms around and smiling."
L.J.  Cherry Valley NY

"There was no mistaking what we saw in the beams of the headlights of our car. When we went back there was nothing there, not even a track in the snow. Years later, Ruth Steenburg who lived at the house at the time often said that there was a little girl that was killed there in a sledding accident many years ago."
J.J.  Cherry Valley NY

"It's funny that you say that because there are many nights I go past there and there is always something that wants to make me stop. It is like something had just crossed the road in front of me."
L.M.  South Valley NY

# The Holt – Moore House   Alden Street

The Holt Farm was one of the earlier farms after the Cherry Valley massacre to be reestablished almost within the village limits. It was a tannery and if you look closely many of the vats are still in the ground at the rear of the house. Overgrown with weeds and filled in, the remains can still be seen. The Young's purchased the farm in the early 1800's, put in new buildings and barns and went into dairy and grain farming. In the early 1900's it became Grand View Farm and the home of P.P. and George Moore who were relatives of the current owners of the property.

---

"I remember my boyfriend waking up in my room and seeing an old lady at the foot of the bed. She nodded to him and disappeared. He was very unsettled and the next morning when I met him for breakfast he related the tale to me. I immediately went to my parent's room and got a picture of great gram, Bessie and brought it to show him. Yes, that was the woman at the foot of the bed."

J.F.  Brooklyn NY

"When I was eight or nine years old there was this little boy who would visit in my room at night. He would just stand at the foot of the bed and stare at me and then he would go. When I moved from that small room to my grandmother's room that is when I started having the feeling of being watched. My friends felt it also and it made them very uncomfortable."

J.F.  Brooklyn NY

"When I was young and lived in Cherry Valley I would walk to my friends' home. They lived in a wonderful old house at the edge of the village. As I came up the walk to the front door, I would always see curtains move as if someone was looking out at me as I approached the house. Several times I saw the figure of an old lady. She was just there, she didn't bother me at all. Another time I saw a little boy sitting on the floor of one of the upstairs bedrooms playing with something on the floor. I could see right through him."

P.H-Y.  Bogue NC

"My brother once told me he saw this lady dressed all in grey walk through the living room and right out the back wall of the house."

J.F.  Brooklyn NY

The Holt – Moore House at the edge of the village.

# The Ashton – Sawyer House  "Lindsay Cottage"
## Campbell Road

Thomas Ashton owned this house in the 1850's. He died in 1871 at the age of seventy-nine years. Now, Thomas was purported to be a loner and never had any family around. He ran a dairy and hop kiln. John Sawyer, publisher of the Cherry Valley Gazette was the next owner of the house sometime in 1918. The house was at one time called *Lindsay Cottage* and was rumored to be part of the Glensfoot farm complex.

---

"We used to have a boy watch our house. He and his dog would check up on the house on a regular basis as we lived in New York City at the time; he lived next door. On this one occasion he met us in the driveway as we were unpacking our car and told us that he could not watch our house anymore as it was haunted and that he was scared to go into the house again.

He told us that he and his dog always inspected the bottom floor of the house and then went to the second floor. On this particular day he went up the stairs and at the top of the landing is as far as the dog would go. The dog's hackles rose and he started growling. Thinking that some sort of animal was in the room at the far end of the hallway he walked down the hallway and opened the door. He confronted a hideous apparition. He and the dog left in one heck of a hurry."

J.S.  Cherry Valley NY

"My sister was staying with me one weekend and she was up all night with the sound of someone walking the hall. She asked me in the morning why I was up all night. I told her I had slept like a log."

B.I.  Cherry Valley NY

"One evening we were sitting on the porch and we heard this loud crash. A mirror that was hanging on the wall in the room at the end of the hallway had crashed to the floor. The nail was still in the wall and the wire holding the mirror was totally intact. It was as if the mirror just jumped off the wall. It was interesting to note that when my daughter and her date came home they told us that they had this incredible urge to talk about the ghost in that upstairs room and so they spent some of the evening swapping stories. That was at nine pm, the same time the mirror came crashing down to the floor."

J.S.  Cherry Valley NY

"I have just experienced the usual creaking and groaning of an old house plus the normal car keys missing and then they show up again in unusual places like potted with one of my houseplants or in the fish tank...you know, just the usual things!"

B.I. Cherry Valley NY

"I have had several guests go to the bathroom during the night and comment to me the next morning about the strange light at the end of the hall. Thank God they didn't open that door at the end of the hall."

J.S. Cherry Valley NY

The Ashton – Sawyer House "Lindsay Cottage"

# William Campbell House   Montgomery Street

Across the road from the Samuel Morse House on Montgomery Street is the Campbell Law Office and the home of Dr. William Campbell, son of Colonel Samuel of Revolutionary War fame. Constructed sometime between 1809 and 1812, the house was built onto an original stone building which dates from the time of the Cherry Valley Massacre. It is believed that the stone building was once a residence and where, on the morning of the Massacre of 1778 it housed several of the soldiers from the fort. Legend has it that the officers met their deaths on the front lawn of the property where they were scalped after being dragged from the house. The front lawn is now where the east wing of the house stands today.

Dr. William studied law and then went into medicine but became more famous as a civil engineer and surveyor than a physician. He was very interested in science so when his friend Samuel F.B. Morse was perfecting his electromagnet for his telegraph machine, the good doctor and his close friends, Dr. Johnson and Amos Swan, a local undertaker, coffin maker and owner of the Cherry Valley Melodeon Company were there to lend a hand. In the 1820's the home had a doctor's office on the ground floor and an apothecary and laboratory in the basement. Now this is where the interesting stories come in. It seems that the good doctor and his friends were very impressed in Morse's electromagnet. They would retire for the evening into the basement laboratory and perform some rather bizarre experiments, such as electrical shock therapy on cadavers in an attempt to bring them back to life. Now, the neighborhood kids used to peek into the cellar from the outside basement windows while these experiments were going on. They could see the blue sparks flying all over the place.

Dr. William Campbell maintained his doctor's office where he lived until 1850. Brayton Campbell occupied the house next followed by Franklin Gorham, a Campbell descendant who was a northern sympathizer from Kentucky. It is rumored that it is he who ran the Underground Railroad in this area. There is a local story that Gorham escaped the *firing* of his home in Kentucky when an angry mob surrounded the house and wanted to burn it down with the *Northern Yankee Trash* inside the dwelling. He and his family escaped and lived in the Campbell house until the close of the Civil War.

In 1903, the Harriott's and several more generations of Campbells held ownership of the house. It stood empty from 1950 to 1966 and then the property was purchased by William Campbell Waldron. The Waldron's were the ones who tore off the large wrap-a-round-porch on the front of the house in 1966.

---

"There are some serious noises that used to come from the kitchen but most of the time it would sound like a party was going on in that room. I just ignored it. Let them have their fun and their memories."

S.W. Gettysburg PA

"I went over to the house for a visit with my baby sitter and we stayed in another room from the adults. We were given all kinds of toys and I remember waking up with the sensation of someone tickling my feet. There was no one there."

J.F. Brooklyn NY

"We had a séance one time up in the attic. This was in the 1970's. The ghost that showed up was a soldier from the sixth Massachusetts Regiment of Colonel Alden and he was pissed off. He said he was an officer from Vermont and that it was Alden's fault that he was killed and that others would not have been killed if Alden had only heeded the warnings of the scouts. The Indians brought them outside of the house and killed them on the front lawn which is where the south wing of the house stands now."

S.W. Gettysburg PA

"I had a friend of mine stay over for an evening and he woke up during the night to the sensation of his feet being tickled. The next thing he knew he was being unceremoniously yanked out of bed. He was very upset. Another time another friend of mine who was sleeping in the front of the house was woken up during the night to someone playing the piano. I never heard a thing."

M.S. Trumensburg NY

"The only time I had to go to the hospital is the time when I was in the study, which is in the east wing of the house. It was dark and I had no lights on. I got up and went to go into the hallway to the kitchen. Something clobbered me. I crumpled to the floor and my wife found me. She took me to the hospital with this huge gash in my forehead. The physician who attended me asked me how it happened. When I told him, I didn't know he told me that the wound on my forehead looked like someone had tried to kill me with an ax."

S.W. Gettysburg PA

"Another friend of mine stayed in the rear bedroom where there are two single beds set up. In the missile of the night she heard heavy footsteps between her and the bed on the other side of her. She freaked and ran out of the room."

S.W. Gettysburg PA

"They used to hide slaves in the hidden stairway in the wall of the house during the Civil War."

C.G.  Cherry Valley NY

"One time I was there all alone. I was sitting in the study reading. All of a sudden, every door in the place slammed shut all at once. It took me a long time to get out of my chair and go investigate. I was really scared."

S.W.  Gettysburg PA

"I live in the apartment over the kitchen area of the house. One night just after my grandmother passed she came to visit me. I was sleeping and was rather annoyed at how she made her appearance. My grandmother lived in the house for many, many years and was a very heavy smoker. The first thing I noticed was the heavy smell of cigarette smoke and then both doors in the apartment flew open. I sighed and said, "Not now Gram, I'm sleeping." The doors shut and the cigarette smell vanished. I went back to sleep."

J.G.  Cherry Valley NY

"While researching this house, some intriguing information came up on Dr. Campbell in one of the archives of a large, local hospital. Dr Campbell made copious, detailed notes on some of his experiments. These notes were inherited by a family member and several generations later they were donated to the hospital. The notes on the experiments using the electromagnet were of particular interest to me as these were noted as possibly being some of the first experiments where the use of electric shock therapy was explored in treating both mental and physical illness."

S.M-M.  Cherry Valley NY

William Campbell House

# Suicide Ridge    Dietsche Road

Suicide Ridge or Tragedy Hill as some prefer to call it, is a part of East Hill that is intersected by Dietsche Road and parallels Rte. 166 all the way to Roseboom. As you drive the road to the top of the ridge on Dietsche Road you are in an area of East Hill where there have been an uncanny number of deaths and strange disappearances. The Hambleton Family farmed the top of this ridge in the 1850's followed by the Dietsche Family in the 1900's.

There once were two gold mines that operated on top of the ridge. The owners used to say they were old diggings and were mined by the Indians many years ago. One was run by a Paul Fuegman and the other was the operation of Earl Welch. The story goes that the gold mine was a cover-up for an illegal still operation.

Earl Welch cut his throat in 1931, a woman committed suicide in his house, her husband's body was found under one of the barns, two young men, one a member of the Dietsche family shot themselves near there and another man walled himself up in a cave near the property and took poison. Neighbors found his body ten years after he disappeared. The Welch and Fuegman Farms are no longer standing up on the ridge but the house and buildings of the Dietsche Farm remain to this day.

Suicide Hill from Rte. 166. A deceptively beautiful area.

"I was born just over the hill near Roseboom, ninety years ago. We bought this farm in 1968 and I remember people saying that the hill in back of our barn was known as Suicide Hill. A boy shot himself while sitting on a rock in the back of our barn in the forties. A woman hung herself in the Welch house not too far from the farmstead here and there was a body found under the floor boards of that same house. Another body was found in a cave on the north side of the ridge."

M.H. Cherry Valley NY

"My dad used to say that the ghost of the *White Lady* was a girl who was murdered up there on top of the hill. It is almost as if she is running from someone. He told me she had something to do with the old gold mine operation. As kids, we used to visit the old farmstead. It was creepy up there, as if someone was always watching you and whatever it was, was evil; really evil."

R.S. Cherry Valley NY

"They found a man's body in the old cave on our property. No one knew who he was at the time, so they just walled up the entrance to the cave with concrete and left him there. He's still up there far as I know."

T.H. Cherry Valley NY

"Some of my family met their end on that hill up there. One by suicide and one mysteriously disappeared until someone found his body stashed under the floorboards of the old house. Several more people disappeared, never to be heard from again. Then there is this story of the strange dog that comes and goes up there. Mean thing, ugly as hell and vicious. He appeared in the village one time with, what some called human remains hanging from his jaws. No one could figure out who he belonged to at the time. That was fifty years ago, and people still see him to this day. I'm sure a dog like that wouldn't go by the name of Fluff or Fido!"

R.W. Cherry Valley

The Dietsche Barn still stands sentential over the ridge known as Suicide Hill.

# Rowley - Webb - Hall House  County Rte. 54  Chestnut Street

The old hop barn is gone as well as the small barn on the side of the house. The rear wall of the house is down into the cellar but the front still stands, giving its best side to the road that once was the only way into Cherry Valley from the east; the Great Western Turnpike. It was a proud house in its time but now it watches you as you go by. Mrs. Ann Rowley lived here in the 1850's and farmed twenty-five acres by herself. She finally sold the place in the 1870's. Mr. Webb died here as did a son and two others; all by suicide. Families have attempted to live in the house but no one does for long, for this is a place that wants to be left alone with its disturbing memories and it is not quiet about letting you know either.

---

"I always remember people telling me it was the *Suicide House* because of the number of deaths that occurred there. It is not only in the house where the creepy feelings are but the grounds around it where the old barns were at one time."

L.J.  Cherry Valley NY

"A few of us kids went in there once. Never again. Every time I think of that experience my hair stands on end."

B.P.  Oneonta NY

"My friend lived there for a time, maybe two years. He used to tell me stories. Once, he was sleeping in his bed and the bed began to shake violently. He called his dad who told him it was just vibrations from Rte. 20 and to go back to sleep.
There was a room on the second floor that no one would go in. There was a cot in that room and that cot was covered in a black cloth, like a shroud. The light in that room kept going on no matter who turned it off. His family even took the bulb out of the socket but there would still be a light in that room. He and his brothers would see the light shining from underneath the crack at the bottom of the door when they went to bed at night."

L.J.  Cherry Valley NY

"We had baby sitters but most refused to come back after the first time. One sitter answered the door one evening after hearing a knock. There stood a man in a red checkered coat. He was definitely weirdly dressed. She glanced back into the house as she didn't quite know what to do and she was very nervous by his appearance. When she looked back, he was not there. When my parents got home they noticed that there were tracks in the snow that led off to the side of the house, but the tracks disappeared at the wood shed."

J.W.  Cobleskill NY

"I just feel that one or more of the suicide victims is still there and reliving their final days. The anger that's there is palpable and very disturbing. I have always wondered what would drive people to take their lives like that?"

J.C. Cherry Valley NY

"We moved up here in the late 1970's and even then, the place was vacant. There was this old couple, relatives of the Halls who used to mow the lawn but that was all the activity there. My wife, Judy and her mom always picked blackberries in the rear of the house but one night there were lights on in the house. The electric had been shut off for many years at that time and they came home and told me about the lights. I went down and there was nothing there and no lights. I remember this particular afternoon, my uncle and I were sitting on my porch when we heard a baby or something that sounded like a baby's cry from the direction of the house. We jumped in my truck and headed down there. As soon as we came to the house the crying stopped, just like that. Deathly quiet. We turned around and headed back and when we got almost to my house the crying started up again."

A.C. Cherry Valley NY

"I knew the Hall's back in the fifties, but they were all gone by 1961. That house hasn't been lived in since."

B.L. Cherry Valley NY

# More Sightings

## Insights and Antidotes

### Howe – Neil House    Quarry Street

"Well. I can tell you that my house is not haunted but there was one incident that I must tell you about that really freaked me out. You see, we had this elderly neighbor across the street. We always looked in on her and brought her food and helped out as best we could. She was in her late eighties when she passed. The day after the funeral, I was walking past the steps that go into the attic in my house. I was passing from one bedroom into the hallway. I glanced up the stairs and there she sat. I was petrified and spell-bound at the same time. She waved at me and almost in that moment she wasn't there sitting on the steps going to my attic anymore. She just wanted to say *goodbye*, I suppose."

L.A.  Cherry Valley NY

### Webb Farm    Co. Rte. 33

"Dor Webb owned this place last, but this farm has been in the Webb Family for at least three generations. I do remember something really strange that happened when I first moved in here but it hasn't happened since. I woke up one night and there in front of my old clock on the mantle was a face. It was as if the clock had a face and that face looked like Santa only without the beard. It disappeared as soon as I noticed it.

There are cold breezes most of the time in the sitting area of the house. There is one room that was primarily used as a wood shed and that room is the only one that really creeps me out. The house is basically a really comfortable place with all the usual noises; the creaks and groans of an old farmhouse. True, the dog growls every once in a while, and there is the sound of heavy boots on the back stairs and the slamming of doors occasionally; the usual stuff. You get used to it after a while."

L.F.  Cherry Valley NY

### Sawyer House  Maiden Lane

"The one thing I remember when I was living there in the 1970's was the fact that I couldn't keep the light off in the living room. I know other people have had this problem, but it really gets annoying after a while. We even unscrewed the bulb in the lamp; no difference. I realize now that Mr. Sawyer made himself known to one of my children. This I hear many years later. The parent is always the last to know."

J.V.  Cherry Valley NY

### Edwin Judd House    Main Street

"Whoever it is doesn't let you forget that they're there. My mom called her Martha and that's all I know, but she's a real door slammer and she loves to hide things plus she smokes. You can't help but notice her and if you don't, well...things happen."

L.M.  South Valley NY

### Diamond House    Rte. 166

"My sister and I were driving home one evening. It was about eleven p.m. and as we went past the Diamond Place on Rte. 166 there was this woman all in white standing right by the side of the road. She didn't move, she just stood there dressed in this long dress. My sister told me to turn around as she wanted to have another look. I told her no way was I going to turn around."

G.J.T.  Cherry Valley NY

### Scott – Burman House    Ottman Funeral Home    Church Street

"I just remember that when we came here our kids were little and I remember them all saying that they could hear footsteps in the hallway and hear someone moving around in the attic. Over the years this was just an accepted part of the house. As the kids grew older and moved out, the noises stopped. I always thought it was *Old Charlie* just checking up on things, including my children."

M.F.  Cherry Valley NY

### Gilday House    Genesee Street

"Every evening at about the same time there is this rocking sound coming from the attic. It is the sound of someone sitting in a rocker and rocking. We got used to it over time and now it doesn't bother us."

S.C.V.  Cherry Valley NY

"Every time I would do a reconstruction project in the house, I would ask if they liked it. I have had no problems with my demolitions and reconstructions when I did it that way. Ask first and they usually don't mind you doing something to their house. Don't ask them...watch out!"

S.C.V.  Cherry Valley NY

### Sash and Blind Factory    Genesee Street

"I remember playing in that abandoned field and sometimes there would be this mist that would rise out of the creek and all us kids would become disoriented. It was really spooky. The town historian says that is the property where Robert Wales had his sawmill and the sash and blind factory was there also. In the later years it became a feed store but there is definitely something there. It is as if we get transported back in time and we see small windows into the lives of others who were here a long time ago."

### William Wiles Farmstead    Co. Rte. 50

"I know that our daughter used to see a man sitting on our front porch. She was always curious about him and commented on his appearance at times. He would just be sitting there, rocking in his rocking chair. That was a long time ago, but to this day she still mentions it occasionally."

W.W.  East Hill

### Morton Road    East Hill

"When I was a kid, back in the 1960's, my friend Francis moved into a house just down the road from us on Morton Road. No one told the family that the house was haunted. It seemed to be a nice place. It was vacant at the time that his family purchased it plus the price was really cheap. Well, it started as soon as they moved in; the sound of barrels rolling around in the basement. It went on from about one in the morning to sunup and was driving my friend and his mom and dad crazy. As a last desperate measure, the family decided to get the local Catholic priest, Father Bouchard to bless the house.
Father Bouchard came and blessed the house and the barrels were quiet. That is what convinced me that the Catholic Faith was the way to go."

E.H.  Cherry Valley NY

### Livingston Falls    Rte. 54

"I love to go down in that small ravine and visit the falls. In the early times it was a favorite swimming hole for the kids in the town and it's always shady and cool there. There have been evenings when I'm down there quietly sitting and I can just faintly make out the laughter and shrieks from the girls of a long ago picnic and swimming party."

S.M-M.  Cherry Valley NY

### Glensfoot Fields   Livingston Falls    Rte. 54

"I was ten or eleven and my sister was nine when this happened to me. We were going for a summer hike and the plan was to go up the Cherry Valley Creek from the cemetery to the *new school*, a distance of over two miles. My sister, her friend and I started out with our little backpacks in which my mom had packed us lunches. We got to Livingston Falls which is in the middle of Glensfoot Gorge and I decided to go off on my own to do a little exploring as I was getting tired of the company of two silly girls. I told them I would be back soon and they were to continue along the creek and they would not get lost.
I headed back toward a stand of trees which intrigued me. These trees were in the middle of a pasture which was surrounded by a corn field on one side. I started into the corn field and I

got hopelessly lost. No matter how hard I tried, I could not find my way out of that cornfield. I walked and walked and pretty soon I had lost track of time and I was scared and tired. All of a sudden, this guy was there. I recognized him as a British soldier of the Revolutionary War period. He had a kind and sympathetic face and he extended his hand to me. I held onto his hand and he led me out of the corn field and into the pasture. We made our way around the corn field and soon we were at Livingston Falls and I could hear my sister calling my name. The soldier smiled at me, dropped my hand and nodded his head in the direction of my sister and her friend. I started toward the direction my sister and her friend was in and when I looked back in the direction of the soldier, he was gone.

When I got back to my sister, she was really mad. They had walked up to the *new school* and were coming back. I had been gone for over three and a half hours."

S.H. Flatfish MT

Sometimes you meet the nicest and most helpful people in a corn field.

### Doc Rosenthal's House    Main Street

"I remember when we moved in. There were the usual knockings on the door and when you went to open it, no one was there. Our dog used to sit up and beg, as if someone was going to give her a treat. We saw no one. Then one day, my sister was staying over and there was a rocking chair in the spare room where she stayed. Very early the next morning she heard the gentle squeak of the rockers moving. She peaked from beneath the bed covers and there was a woman sitting in the rocking chair rocking back and forth.

My neighbors always told me it was old Mrs. Rosenthal who was haunting the place. She was looking for the Doc. He passed before she did and she lived only a short time longer in the home and then she went to live out her final days in a nursing home. She asked every day where he was."

F.J.W.  Cherry Valley NY

### Catherine Roseboom – Lum House    Montgomery Street

"When I lived in the Lum house, the former residence of Catherine Roseboom noted Cherry Valley philanthropist, I had several experiences with a ghost. It was always the same ghost, a lady wearing a large hat with a very large flower in it.

My oldest child would also see her standing in his doorway or sitting quietly in the corner of his room. I knew it was Mrs. Lum because when I was a kid she always wore big hats with flowers."

S.G.  Cherry Valley NY

"It was always a busy house with comings and goings by us here in this world and with them in their world. It was as if we were living our lives side by side but never seeing one another."

S.G.  Cherry Valley NY

### The Old Episcopal Manse    Montgomery Street

"When I was little I had a friend, who lived at the old manse of the Episcopal Church. We always played down stairs and she told me that she never went upstairs as there were *funny* people up there and she was afraid of them."

C.C.  Conesus NY

"When we lived there, there definitely was a lot of strange things that happened. You would hear footsteps at night and see shadows of people standing in the hallway. You got used to it after a while and it didn't bother you anymore. By the time I moved out, most of the activity was gone. I just think they moved on to where ever they go after they die."

S.W.  Gettysburg PA

### The Limekiln      Alden Street

"Johnny Hamilton was fourteen years old when a wall of the limekiln collapsed in on him, killing him instantly. This accident happened in 1818 and for years after, the ghost of the boy could be seen near the stone walls of the kiln."

S.M-M. Cherry Valley NY

### The Burton Farm      Rte. 166

"It was 1972 and my mon was determined to buy a house in Cherry Valley. She was actively looking at property and when she went and looked at a farm on the outskirts of town, things got very interesting. The house was abandoned at that time and was totally cleaned out with the exception of one upstairs room. The door to the room had a draw bolt on the outside of the door not the inside so someone could easily lock someone in the room. The room was empty with the exception of a picture on the wall. The picture was that of a child and the child's face was gone from the picture. Someone had selectively cut the face out with a scissors. The most interesting thing about the picture was it seemed as if someone was also using it as a dart board.

My mom was very shaken when she saw this and she left the room very quickly. It was foggy out when she went to get in her car. The transparent figure of a man dressed in old farm clothes came out of the fog and yelled for her to "get out." She didn't waste any time in getting out of there."

M.T.S. Cherry Valley NY

### Cherry Valley Fish and Game Club      Fish and Game Road

"I do get a creepy feeling like I'm being watched. This is when I walk from the pond to the parking lot when it's most intense and it's after dark; after I've finished fishing. Never have I felt anything in the club house or any of the out buildings, just the land around the lake and up into the woods going toward Clyde Gulf. And just at night. It's a lovely and serene place in the daytime, but as you approach midnight, there's something there. I just know it has to so with the Massacre, for there's a legend that this was a small farm belonging to a family that never made it out alive on that day."

B.S. Cherry Valley NY

"It is an unspoken rule; you get out of there before ten p.m. But the most intriguing thing is the outside sensor light. Sometimes it works and will light when it's activated and sometimes it leaves everyone in the dark. The annoying thing is that we know the light functions and the switch is turned on. Heck, we even had it checked by an electrician but it just loves to do its own thing."

F.S. Sharon Springs NY

### Dutcher – Weber House     Main Street

"One day I enlisted my best friend to stay with my son overnight as I had to be out of town for a few days. After seeing to my son, my friend retired to the guest bedroom. Sometime after midnight she heard someone slam the back door. Soon after hearing the door slam, she heard heavy footsteps on the stairs. She was terrified. The next thing she knew, she felt someone sitting on her bed and nothing was there. She never stayed overnight again."
L.F.  Cherry Valley NY

### Otsego Motel   Rte. 20

"There was a knock on the door of the house and I opened it and there stood this beautiful young girl. She wore a long, white dress and she had curly hair down to her waist. I don't know why but I wasn't scared as she was obviously a ghost. I simply asked, "Why are you here?" She told me that she needed help. When I asked her, who did this to her she told me that it was her mother. I asked her why and she told me, "because I was pregnant.""
R.H.B.  Seward NY

"When my mom and I ran the place in the late eighties, there were always these unexplained things happening here. But the most unusual ones were the orbs and weird-shaped lights and shadows of crosses on the lawn when there weren't any crosses anywhere around to cast any form of a shadow on the grass. These shadows would just show up on the lawn. Something occurred on this land a long time ago and I have always wondered what it was. This is a pleasant enough place and people liked staying here. It was convenient and we had decent food and all, but the supernatural goings-on always perplexed us."
R.H.B.  Seward NY

Beaker shaped lights appear frequently on the back lawn of the motel.

## Home of Hiram Countryman     Co. Rte. 50

Hiram Countryman farmed eighty-five acres on this property in the 1850's. There is a legend that during the massacre a toddler, one belonging to a Campbell was carried off from this property and that all the barns and the house were destroyed with the family still inside the home. This could account for all the strange sightings in the yard where the original cabin stood.

There are Indian mounds in the backyard and the old millstream that flows over Eacker's Falls flows through the yard. The remains of the old millrace and the foundation of the mill is still visible. There are always sightings in this house but they seem to be different time eras. Weird feelings are always present in the yard after dark and lights and orbs are visible also."

S.M-M. Cherry Valley NY

*I don't want my life to be defined by what is etched on a tombstone. I want it to be defined in what is etched in the lives and hearts of those I've touched.*

Steve Maraboli

"I think that there is an unblemished, spiritual energy here that is primeval and we are a power center for this positive energy in its pure form."

P.W. Cherry Valley NY

"I took my granddaughter to her concert as she was playing in the school band. Her mom had passed about eight years before that evening. I will never forget this, for there was my daughter, as real as life sitting in the audience in the auditorium of the new school watching her daughter play in the band."

D.W. South Valley NY

"My daughter and son-in-law moved into my uncle's home just after he passed. It is a beautiful house and before long my two granddaughters were born. When the oldest granddaughter was about three she used to get out her tea set and every afternoon have tea with her "Uncle Beak." This went on for several years until she found out that school would interfere with her *teatime*. She proudly announced that he told her he would wait for her until school was finished for the day. They still enjoy their tea together, every afternoon after school."

B.H. Pittsburg PA

"I remember when my young grandson passed from an accident. I lay in bed after that funeral, which was probably the worst experience in my life and suddenly I felt a hand on my cheek. It was warm and so very comforting, I didn't want to move. Tears streamed down my face as I felt that hand resting on my cheek. I stayed in the position I was in for at least fifteen minutes or so as I didn't want to move for fear that the feeling would go. As the sensation started to fade I knew it was my grandson just telling me he was ok."

B.D. Cherry Valley NY

"I've never believed in ghosts but there is a time in ones' life when one has to face reality. My new *credo* is, "do you believe in the Holy Spirit?" If you answer yes, then my answer to you is, "then you believe in ghosts.""

L.T. Cherry Valley NY

"Every once-in-a-while I will smell pipe tobacco or a familiar perfume or maybe I feel a caress on the cheek. Sometimes we will get home after an evening out and every light in the house is on. It is just loved ones checking up on me; see if I need anything. That's all."

S.M-M. Cherry Valley NY

I was supposed to go to a family reunion but I just didn't feel like it. My daughter had just passed away and I just didn't feel like I wanted to go anywhere or do anything. I had baked for the event and was going to have my husband deliver what I had baked. I remember being in the kitchen and suddenly the entire area was filled with bright, white light. A very deep feeling of peace came over me and it was as if my daughter was telling me that it was ok to go to the reunion. From that day forward, I believe my daughter is with me always."

D.W. South Valley NY

"This area of New York State is what I call a *lost place*. Time hasn't really touched it at all."

L.M. South Valley NY

"I used to live in a house on Main Street and many times I would see a Revolutionary War Soldier in that house. When I moved, he went with me. I think he was a relative for as soon as I got settled into my new house, he disappeared."

L.F. Cherry Valley NY

"It is like they, the ghosts carry on their lives as they did when they were here. I feel it going on all around me when I am in my house. Life, in whatever form it takes, it is still life. I just love the hustle and bustle, I can feel it and it's a part of my house and their house too."

K.S. Cherry Valley NY

"One night I had a dream and in it my deceased husband came to me. In this dream he was waiting to board a plane. I told him he needed to get on that plane immediately and he told me he had eight minutes in which to board. The dream ended. The next night he comes to me again in a second dream and this time he hands me a pail of tools and tells me I'm going to need them. Seven days later my house burned to the ground."

D.W. South Valley NY

"My granddaughter was just five years old when this happened, but I will never forget it. She had made a very close friendship with an elderly neighbor. There was something spiritual about the way they reacted to one another and it was refreshing to see this bond between a small child and an elderly lady. The lady passed on and as we were walking past her home one day, I casually mentioned to my granddaughter that her friend was now in heaven with my father. I further stated that it was a shame that my granddaughter had never known her grandfather as he had died before she was born. My granddaughter stopped in her tracks, turned and faced me and said in a very stern voice, "I have so. I met him in heaven before I came here, and he gave me a hug.""

B.D. Cherry Valley NY

"I remember my accident as if it were today. I had taken the car to see about a problem my neighbor was having and of course I did not hook up my seatbelt. After all, it was only down the road. There was ice everywhere and as I came over the hill there was a car stopped in the middle of the road. I couldn't stop and so we hit head on. As my body propelled its way toward the steering wheel I remember my entire life being played out before me but in slow motion. Then, in an instant, right in front of me was my Uncle John who had passed away when I was very young. He had his hand out, palm forward as if to shove me back into the seat. I survived. I had many bruises but the most intriguing one was of a hand print right in the middle of my chest."

S.A.R. Cherry Valley NY

"We were all sitting around during *coffee hour* after church and the subject came up about ghosts and in particular the ghost at the old school. It was stated that many thought that the spirit was one of the janitors that used to work there. One of our older parishioners got very indignant and said that she didn't believe in that stuff, that the soul died with the body and that it would go to heaven after the second coming of Christ and that it was not very Christian to think otherwise.

Our parish priest was sitting up at the head of the table enjoying some cake and coffee. The lady went up to him and said something to the effect that the ghost at the school couldn't be a person and that some were speculating that it was the janitor that had once worked there. Father looked at her with a twinkle in his eye and said, "Well, that depends, are they still paying him?"

S.M-M. Cherry Valley NY

"Now I lay me down to sleep,

Pray the Lord my soul to keep..."

18th century children's prayer

# ABOUT THE AUTHOR

Susan Murray-Miller is a writer, photographer, small business owner, Reiki Master, ghost communicator, a dowser and the historian of the Town and Village of Cherry Valley NY. Able to see and hear ghosts and spirits at an early age, she loves to write about her experiences. Susan lives in Cherry Valley in a house built in 1804 with its plethora of resident ghosts. She has four children and two grandchildren.

Susan loves to travel, kayak, hike and photograph besides learning more about the history of her area and the ghosts that inhabit it. She spends her time at her store and with family and friends, writing, clearing houses of unwanted entities as well as lecturing on the subjects of ghosts and the history of the central New York area of Cherry Valley.

www.ingramcontent.com/pod-product-compliance
Lightning Source LLC
LaVergne TN
LVHW061224060426
835509LV00012B/1420